# THE MARE'S TRAP

# THE MARE'S TRAP

## Nature and Culture in the *Kamasutra*

Wendy Doniger

SPEAKING TIGER

SPEAKING TIGER PUBLISHING PVT. LTD
4381/4, Ansari Road, Daryaganj
New Delhi 110002

First published by Speaking Tiger 2015



ISBN: 978-93-85288-06-7
eISBN: 978-93-85288-07-4

10 9 8 7 6 5 4 3 2 1



Typeset in Adobe Garamond Pro by SÜRYA, New Delhi
Printed at Sanat Printers, Kundli

# CONTENTS

# INTRODUCTION

## REDEEMING THE *KAMASUTRA*

Two things happened to change my mind about the *Kamasutra* since I wrote some of the early essays on which this book is based.[i]

First of all, I began reading Kautilya's *Arthashastra* again for a new project, and I saw for the first time how closely Vatsyayana's *Kamasutra* is based upon it. This insight led to a new chapter,[ii] but it also coloured all my other perceptions of the *Kamasutra*; it's surprising how many of the puzzles in the *Kamasutra* are resolved when you realize that it is based on the *Arthashastra*. These new insights led me to revise the older essays in the volume, and to my surprise and delight they formed a new book, like pieces of a broken vase in a film that you run backwards to form a whole vase again. The unifying theme was the tension between nature and culture.[iii]

The second thing that changed my understanding of the *Kamasutra* was the rise of a wave of puritanical censorship in India in the past decade. Small but noisy political and religious groups have objected not only to works of art (paintings, books, films) that dealt with aspects of sexuality, but to any public demonstration of desire, even to young

---

i Chapters one, three, four, five and seven.

ii Chapter two, 'The Kautilyan *Kamasutra*'.

iii Chapter six, 'The Mare's Trap'.

(heterosexual) couples holding hands in public.[iv] This made me realize how important it was to try to remind contemporary Indian readers that the *Kamasutra* was an occasion for national pride, not national shame, that it was a great and wise book, not a dirty book. Hence the present volume.

Just recently I happened to stumble across the passage in the *Malatimadhava* (by the eighth century CE playwright Bhavabhuti) in which a woman in private conversation with other women, one of whom has been raped on her wedding night, casually cites the *Kamasutra* verse warning men to be gentle with their brides, lest the women learn to hate sex.[1] It made me realize yet again how well-known the *Kamasutra* had been in India in earlier times, right up to and through the reign of the Mughals, who had had it translated into Persian and had commissioned lavishly illustrated Persian and Sanskrit *Kamasutra* manuscripts. I had hoped that making the text available, in 2002, in a contemporary translation,[2] devoid of the prurient Orientalism that marred Sir Richard Burton's translation, would help to resurrect the *Kamasutra* as a serious book about the sophisticated, cosmopolitan *beau monde* of ancient India. But now, over a decade later, though the new translation has made a mark throughout Europe,[3] the *Kamasutra* is still rarely discussed in India by anyone who has read it. Never one to give up without a fight, I am hoping that *The Mare's Trap* will have better luck in restoring the *Kamasutra* to its proper place in the Sanskrit canon and, indeed, in the honour role of the literary landmarks of the great Indian heritage.

---

iv Chapter seven, 'The Rise and Fall of Kama and the *Kamasutra*'.

### THE COURAGE OF THE *KAMASUTRA*

Even in its day, and despite its popularity in many sectors of the ancient Indian world, the *Kamasutra* had to fight against elements of Hinduism that regarded sex with an ambivalence that was to be rivalled only by that of the nineteenth century Victorians (such as Burton[v]). As an example of the unique courage of the *Kamasutra*, consider the way that Vatsyayana challenges the basic dharma of fertility. Where the *Dharmashastra* of Manu says that a man has a duty to have sex with his wife during her fertile period,[4] and the *Mahabharata* and Puranas abound in stories of men who either go to great lengths to fulfil this duty or are punished for neglecting it, Vatsyayana dismisses with one or two short sentences the possibility that the purpose of the sexual act might be to produce children;[vi] for the rest of the book, he ignores fertility entirely and is concerned only with the sexual goal of pleasure (one of the primary meanings of kama). Similarly, Vatsyayana's completely non-judgmental attitude to sexual acts between two men[vii] was even more daring in his day than it was in ours until very recently indeed.

But by far the most significant of Vatsyayana's acts of defiance of dharma is his attitude to adultery. Manu regards adultery as a legal crime, as does the *Arthashastra*,[5] though they differ about the punishment of the adulterous couple. Manu says, 'If a woman who is proud of her relatives or her

v See chapter five, 'The Third Nature', and chapter seven, 'The Rise and Fall of Kama and the *Kamasutra*'.

vi See chapter four, 'Women in the *Kamasutra*'.

vii See chapter five, 'The Third Nature'.

own qualities deceives her husband with another man, the king should have her eaten by dogs in a place frequented by many people. And he should have the evil man burnt on a red-hot iron bed, and people should pile wood on it, and the evil-doer should be burnt up.'[6] The *Arthashastra* is only slightly more lenient, though less imaginative:[7] 'If the husband were to forgive her, both [the woman and her lover] should be set free. If she is not forgiven, the woman's ears and nose should be cut off, and her paramour shall be put to death.'[8]

None of this is in the *Kamasutra*, which devotes a whole book (Book Five) to minute and psychologically acute instructions to the man who wishes to commit adultery, detailing hundreds of stratagems by which he may sleep with the wives of other men. But Vatsyayana pulls back at the very end with verses warning the man not to do it, and to guard his own wife:

> A man who knows texts and considers, from the text,
> the devices whose tell-tale signs are detailed
> in the discussion of the seduction of other men's wives,
> is never deceived by his own wives.
> But he himself should never seduce other men's wives,
> because these techniques show only one of the two sides of
> each case, because the dangers are clearly visible,
> and because it goes against both dharma and artha.
> This book was undertaken in order
> to guard wives, for the benefit of men;
> its arrangements should not be learned
> in order to corrupt the people.[9]

In the light of all that has preceded this passage in the rest of the chapter, we might be inclined to dismiss it as mere hypocrisy, an attempt to avoid possible prosecution for preaching a doctrine directly contrary to Indian law at the time.

But there is other, more subtle evidence that Vatsyayana may be more genuinely conflicted about adultery. Even when the *Kamasutra* tells stories that the go-between is instructed to tell to the target woman in order to persuade her to betray her husband, the actual content of the stories is better designed to warn her off, as the women in the stories invariably suffer and/or come to a bad end.[viii] The stories, like the verses, are taken from an older, moralistic corpus; the new material contradicts it. But which one expresses Vatsyayana's own opinion?

## IF FREUD HAD MET VATSYAYANA

Sigmund Freud had a great deal to say about sexual ambivalence, and if Freud had met Vatsyayana, and analysed him for us, he might well have helped us to decode what Vatsyayana was censoring, both consciously (in order to avoid running afoul of the enforcers of dharma) and unconsciously (in his own mixed feelings about much of what his goal of totality[ix] forced him to write about). On the other hand, the chronology of the lives of Freud and Burton does allow for the historical possibility that Freud might have had the opportunity to analyse Burton's ambivalent sexuality:[x] Burton lived from 1821 to 1890, Freud from

---

viii See chapter three, 'The Mythology of Kama'.

ix See chapter five, 'The Third Nature'.

x See chapter five, 'The Third Nature' and chapter seven, 'The Rise and Fall of Kama and the *Kamasutra*'.

1856 to 1939. Therefore in 1890, when Burton, at the end of his life, was sixty-nine, Freud was thirty-four, and had been pursuing his research in 'nervous disorders' for five years; he might easily have made the trip from Vienna to London...We will, alas, never know.

In any case, I think Vatsyayana knew more about sex than Freud did (and certainly more than Burton did). You don't need Freud to understand the sexual symbolism of the *Kamasutra*,[xi] nor to appreciate the self-deceptions that drive the man-about-town in his pursuit of women. And I doubt that Freud would be of much use in helping us to understand the deep post-colonial insecurities and religious ambivalences that are keeping contemporary Indians from appreciating the *Kamasutra*. I think Vatsyayana is the only one who can inspire them to overcome their self-doubts and rejoice in this great cultural masterpiece.

---

xi See chapter six, 'The Mare's Trap'.

# 1

# THE STRANGE AND THE FAMILIAR IN THE *KAMASUTRA*[1]

The *Kamasutra* is the oldest extant Indian textbook of erotic love, and one of the oldest in the world. There is nothing remotely like it even now, and for its time it was astonishingly sophisticated; it was already well-known in India at a time when the Europeans were still swinging in trees, culturally (and sexually) speaking.

The *Kamasutra* was composed in Sanskrit, the literary language of ancient India,[2] probably sometime in the second half of the third century of the Common Era, in North India, perhaps in Pataliputra (near the present city of Patna, in Bihar). The two words in its title mean 'desire/love/pleasure/sex' (*kama*) and 'a treatise' (*sutra*). Virtually nothing is known about the author, Vatsyayana Mallanaga, other than his name and what little we learn from the text. Nor do we know anything about Yashodhara, who wrote the definitive commentary on the *Kamasutra,* in the thirteenth century, a text called the *Jayamangala*. But Vatsyayana tells us something important about his text, namely, that it is a distillation of the works of a number of authors who preceded him, authors whose texts have not come down to us. Vatsyayana cites them often—sometimes in agreement, sometimes in disagreement—though his own voice always comes through, as ringmaster over the many acts he incorporates in his sexual circus.

Most people think the *Kamasutra* is a book about the positions (often improbable) in sexual intercourse, the erotic counterpart to the ascetic asanas of yoga. Reviews of books dealing with the *Kamasutra* in recent years have had titles like 'Assume the Position' and 'Position Impossible'. *Cosmopolitan* magazine published two editions of its 'Cosmo *Kamasutra*', offering '12 brand-new mattress-quaking sex styles', each with its numerical 'degree of difficulty', including positions called 'the backstairs boogie', 'the octopus', 'the mermaid', 'the spider web' and 'the rock'n'roll'.[3] One website offered *The Kamasutra of Pooh*, posing stuffed animals in compromising positions (Piglet on Pooh, Pooh mounting Eeyore, and so forth). Palm Pilot had a copyrighted 'Pocket Sutra: The Kama Sutra in the palm of your hand', which offered 'lying down positions', 'sitting positions', 'rear-entry positions', 'standing positions', 'role reversal' and many more. There is a *Kamasutra* wristwatch that displays a different position every hour. More seriously, Roland Barthes, in *The Pleasure of the Text*, took the *Kamasutra* as a root metaphor for literary as well as physical desire: 'The text you write must prove to me that it desires me. This proof exists: it is writing. Writing is: the science of the various blisses of language, its *Kama Sutra* (this science has but one treatise: writing itself).'[4] The text for sex is thus the sex of the text, too.

The part of the *Kamasutra* describing the positions may have been the best-thumbed passage in previous ages of sexual censorship, but nowadays, when sexually explicit novels, films and instruction manuals are widely available, that part is the least useful. The *real Kamasutra* is a book about the art of living—about finding a partner, maintaining power in a marriage, committing adultery, living as or with a courtesan, using drugs—and also about the positions in sexual intercourse. The *Kamasutra* was certainly not the first of its genre, nor was it the last. But the many textbooks of eroticism that follow it, such as the *Kokashastra* (or *Ratirahasya*) and the *Anangaranga*, eliminate most of the *Kamasutra*'s encyclopaedic social and psychological narratives and concentrate primarily on the sexual positions, of which they describe many more than are found in the *Kamasutra*.

## CLASS IN THE *KAMASUTRA*

Whom was it written for? It is difficult to assess how broad a spectrum of ancient Indian society knew the text first-hand. It would be good to have more information about social conditions in India at the time of the composition of the *Kamasutra*, but the *Kamasutra* itself is one of the main sources that we have for such data; the text is, in a sense, its own context. The world of the *Kamasutra* is a world of privilege; the lovers must be rich. Much of the *Kamasutra* is about culture, which belonged to those who had leisure and means, time and money, none of which was in short supply for the text's primary intended audience, an urban (and urbane) elite consisting of princes, high state officials and wealthy merchants.

The *Kamasutra* is almost unique in classical Sanskrit literature in its near total disregard of class (*varna*) and caste (*jati*). Of course, power relations of many kinds—gender, wealth, political position, as well as caste—are implicit throughout the text. But wealth is what counts most. The lovers must be rich, not necessarily upper-class. When the text says that the man may get his money from 'gifts, conquest, trade, or wages, or from inheritance, or from both,' the commentator (Yashodhara), a thousand years later, explains, 'If he is a Brahmin, he gets his money from gifts; a king or warrior, from conquest; a commoner, from trade; and a servant, from wages earned by working as an artisan, a travelling bard, or something of that sort.'[5]

*Varna* and *jati,* class and caste, are mentioned just a few times, once in a single sentence admitting that class is of concern only when you marry a wife who will bear you legal sons, and can be disregarded in all other erotic situations;[6] once when the go-between is advised to tell the target woman stories about 'other virgins of equal caste' [*jati*[7]]; and later in a discussion of possible sexual partners:

> 'Sex with a coarse servant' takes place with a lower-class female water-carrier or house-servant, until the climax; in this kind of sex, he does not bother with the acts of civility. Similarly, 'sex with a peasant' takes place between a courtesan and a country bumpkin, until the climax, or between a man-about-town and women from the countryside, cow-herding villages, or countries beyond the borders.[8]

Vatsyayana disapproves of sexual relations with rural and tribal women because they could have adverse effects on the erotic refinement and sensibility of the cultivated man-about-town; he would have been baffled by any Lady Chatterji's sexual transports with a gamekeeper. But for all the rest of the discussion of pleasure, class is irrelevant—or, perhaps, understood without having to be mentioned. Where classical texts of Hindu social law might have said that you make love differently to women of high and low classes, Vatsyayana just says that you make love differently to women of delicate or rough temperaments; money matters, but status does not.

## THE LIFE OF A MAN-ABOUT-TOWN

The world of the *Kamasutra* is a fantasized world of sex that is in many ways the prototype for Hugh Hefner's glossy *Playboy* empire. The privilege of the *Kamasutra* lovers is expressed in the opulence of the instructions on the home decorating of the ideal lover. The protagonist of the *Kamasutra*, literally a 'man-about-town' (*nagaraka*, from the Sanskrit *nagara*, city), lives 'in a city, a capital city, a market town, or some large gathering where there are good people, or wherever he has to stay to make a living'.[9] He has, as we say of a certain type of man today, no visible means of support. His companions may have quite realistic money problems;[10] his wife is entrusted with all the household management, including the finances; and his mistresses work hard to make and keep their money. But we never see the man-about-town at work.

This is how he spends a typical day:

> First is his morning toilet: He gets up in the morning, relieves himself, cleans his teeth, applies fragrant oils in small quantities, as well as incense, garlands, bees' wax and red lac, looks at his face in a mirror, takes some mouthwash, and attends to the things that need to be done. He bathes every day, has his limbs rubbed with oil every second day, a foam bath every third day, his face shaved every fourth day, and his body hair removed every fifth or tenth day. All of this is done without fail. And he continually cleans the sweat from his armpits. In the morning and afternoon he eats.[11]

Yashodhara's commentary explains the reasons behind some of these details:

> He uses oil in small quantities, because he is no man-about-town if he uses large amounts. He colours his lips with a ball of moist red lac and fixes it with a small ball of bees' wax. He puts a ball of sweet-smelling mouthwash in his cheek and takes some betel in his hand to use later. He has the hair shaved from his hidden place with a razor every fifth day, and then, every tenth day, has his body hair pulled out by the roots, because it grows so fast. The sweat that breaks out after any activity must be constantly removed with a rag, to prevent a bad smell and a consequent lack of sophistication.

Now, ready to face the day, he goes to work:

> After eating, he passes the time teaching his parrots and mynah birds to speak; goes to quail-fights, cockfights and ram-fights; engages in various arts and games; and passes the time with his libertine, pander and clown. And he takes a nap. In the late afternoon, he gets dressed up and goes to salons to amuse himself. And in the evening, there is music and singing. After that, on the bed in a bedroom carefully decorated and perfumed by sweet-smelling incense, he and his friends await the women who are slipping out for a rendezvous with them. He sends female messengers for them or goes to get them himself. And when the women arrive, he and his friends greet them with gentle conversation and courtesies that charm the mind and heart. If rain has soaked the clothing of women who have slipped out for a rendezvous in bad weather, he changes their clothes himself, or gets some of his friends to serve them. That is what he does by day and night.[12]

Busy teaching his birds to talk, he never drops in to check things at the shop, let alone visit his mother. Throughout the text, his one concern is the pursuit of pleasure. Well, there were undoubtedly men (and women) in ancient India who had that sort of money and the privilege that came with it; Sanskrit literature tells us, in particular, of wealthy merchants whose sons engaged in the sorts of adventures, erotic and otherwise, that other literatures often reserve for princes.[13] Vatsyayana insists that anyone, not just the man-about-town, can live the life of pleasure—if he or she has money.[14]

That is not to say, however, that the pursuit of pleasure didn't require its own work. Vatsyayana details the sixty-four arts that need to be learned by anyone (male or female) who is truly serious about pleasure:

> singing; playing musical instruments; dancing; painting; cutting leaves into shapes; making lines on the floor with rice-powder and flowers; arranging flowers; colouring the teeth, clothes and limbs; making jewelled floors; preparing beds; making music on the rims of glasses of water; playing water sports; unusual techniques; making garlands and stringing necklaces; making diadems and headbands; making costumes; making various earrings; mixing perfumes; putting on jewellery; doing conjuring tricks; practising sorcery; sleight of hand; preparing various forms of vegetables, soups and other things to eat; preparing wines, fruit juices and other things to drink; needlework; weaving; playing the lute and the drum; telling jokes and riddles; completing words; reciting difficult words; reading aloud; staging plays and dialogues; completing verses; making things out of cloth, wood and cane; woodworking; carpentry; architecture; the ability to test gold and silver;

> metallurgy; knowledge of the colour and form of jewels; skill at nurturing trees; knowledge of ram-fights, cockfights and quail-fights; teaching parrots and mynah birds to talk; skill at rubbing, massaging and hairdressing; the ability to speak in sign language; understanding languages made to seem foreign; knowledge of local dialects; skill at making flower carts; knowledge of omens; alphabets for use in making magical diagrams; alphabets for memorizing; group recitation; improvising poetry; knowledge of dictionaries and thesauruses; knowledge of metre; literary work; the art of impersonation; the art of using clothes for disguise; special forms of gambling; the game of dice; children's games; etiquette; the science of strategy; and the cultivation of athletic skills.[15]

And while we are still reeling from this list, Vatsyayana immediately reminds us that there is, in addition, an entirely different cluster of sixty-four arts of love,[16] which include eight forms of each of the main erotic activities: embracing, kissing, scratching, biting, sexual positions, moaning, the woman playing the man's part and oral sex.[17] A rapid calculation brings the tab to 128 arts, a curriculum that one could hardly master even after the equivalent of two Ph.Ds and a long apprenticeship; not many could afford it. Clearly the *Kamasutra* was intended to be useful mainly for the man-about-town—and, indeed, the woman-about-town.[i]

## THE *KAMASUTRA* AS A PLAY

What is its genre? Beneath the veneer of a sexual textbook, the *Kamasutra* resembles a work of dramatic fiction more

---

i See chapter four, 'Women in the *Kamasutra*'.

than anything else. The man and woman whose sex lives are described here are called the hero and heroine, and the men who assist the hero are called the libertine, pander and clown. All of these are terms for stock characters in Sanskrit dramas—the hero and heroine, sidekick, supporting player and jester. Is the *Kamasutra* a play about sex? Certainly it has a dramatic sequence, and, like most classical Indian dramas, it has seven acts. In Act One, which literally sets the stage for the drama, the bachelor sets up his pad; in Act Two, he perfects his sexual technique. Then he seduces a virgin (Act Three), gets married and lives with a wife or wives (Act Four); tiring of her (or them), he seduces other men's wives (Act Five); and when he tires of that, he frequents courtesans (Act Six). Finally, when he is too old to manage it at all, he resorts to aphrodisiacs and magic spells (Act Seven).

## THE *KAMASUTRA* AND THE CONTEMPORARY READER

The *Kamasutra* is firmly situated within the value system of what might be called the ancient 'Indian way'; it shares many of its unstated assumptions with those of traditional Indian texts. And yet, it is also a unique text, unusual for its time—closer, in some ways, to ours.

Two worlds in the *Kamasutra* intersect for contemporary readers, both Indian and non-Indian: sex and ancient India. We assume that the understanding of sex will be familiar to us, since sex is universal, and that the representations of ancient India will be strange to us, since that world existed long ago and (for non-Indians) in a galaxy far away. This is largely the case, but there are interesting reversals of expectations: some sexual matters are strange (for Vatsyayana argues that sex for human beings is a matter of culture, not nature[ii]), or even sometimes repugnant, to us today; while some cultural matters are strangely familiar or, if unfamiliar, still charming and comprehensible, reassuring us that the people of ancient India were in many ways just like contemporary readers. Consider the description of the man's day: his morning toilet is much like ours, but we do not, alas, schedule in things like teaching mynah birds to speak. It is the constant intersection of these perceptions—'How very odd!', 'Oh, I know just how she feels!'—that constitutes the strange appeal of the *Kamasutra*.

Many readers will recognize the man who tells the woman on whom he's set his sights 'about an erotic dream, pretending that it was about another woman',[18] and the woman who does the same thing.[19] Others will feel a guilty pang of familiarity when reading the passage suggesting that a woman interested in getting a man's attention in a crowded room might find some pretext to take something from him, making sure to brush him with her breast as she reaches across him.[20] This is an amazingly intimate thing to know about a culture, far more intimate than knowing that you can stand on one leg or another when you make love. Sometimes the unfamiliar and the familiar are cheek-by-jowl: the culture-specific list of women the wife must not associate with, which includes a Buddhist nun and a magician who uses love-sorcery worked with roots,[21] is followed in the very next passage by the woman who is cooking for her man and finds out 'this is what he likes, this is what he

ii See chapter seven, 'The Mare's Trap'.

hates, this is good for him, this is bad for him', a consideration that must resonate with many contemporary readers, cooking for someone they love, balancing the desire to please (perhaps with a Béarnaise sauce? Or a curry made with lots of ghee?) with the concern for the rising cholesterol level.

In the realm of culture, too, there are moments that travel well across the centuries from Vatsyayana's time to ours. There is the charming item, in the Borgesian list of arts, of making music on the rims of glasses of water, something that people do nowadays, too. There is the passage in which the boy teases the girl when they are swimming together, diving down and coming up near her, touching her, and then diving down again;[22] this is familiar territory for me, at least; it was already an old trick when I was a young girl at summer camp in the Adirondacks, and boys would do this sort of thing. On the other hand, the magic formulas used to enhance penis size[iii] remain truly foreign to people of the twenty-first century; a comparison with Viagra is superficially useful here, but it does not get you far enough to take this part of the text seriously on its own terms. Magic and drugs, the life in the harem, the world of courtesans—these parts of the *Kamasutra* make you think, 'How very different these people are from us.' Or, as a Victorian gentleman cited by Hilaire Belloc remarked after seeing Shakespeare's *Antony and Cleopatra*, 'How different, how very different, from the home life of our own dear Queen.'

For South Asians, there are bits of the text that are startlingly familiar from the everyday world of India today. For people who grew up elsewhere, these become accessible

iii See chapter six, 'The Mare's Trap'.

only through rather distant analogies. Betel, for instance, *tambula*, nowadays called paan, is still popular across India (though not used quite in the manner, or for the purpose, prescribed by Vatsyayana). It is a delicacy made of a betel leaf rolled up around a paste made of areca nuts (sometimes called betel nuts), cardamom, lime paste and other flavours, sometimes with tobacco or other stimulants (including, sometimes, cocaine). The finished product, shaped rather like a stuffed grape-leaf, is eaten as a stimulant, to redden the mouth and to freshen the breath. Throughout the *Kamasutra*, lovers give one another betel, take betel out of their own mouths and put it in their lover's mouth. This basic part of the erotic scene in ancient India can best be understood by non-Indians through an analogy with the overtones that champagne has, or the post-coital cigarette. (A closer analogy, perhaps, is supplied by the recurrent scene in *Now, Voyager* [1942], in which Paul Henreid lights two cigarettes in his mouth and hands one to Bette Davis.)

The woman's thoughts on such subjects as how to keep a lover[23] and how to tell when his affections are cooling[24] ring remarkably true for the twenty-first century reader, regardless of his or her culture. Another part of the text that surely speaks to the modern reader is the description of a man who wants to seduce a married woman. In the would-be adulterer's meditations on reasons to do this, there are self-deceptive arguments that still make sense in our world:

> He thinks: 'There is no danger involved in my having this woman, and there is a chance of wealth. And since I am useless, I have exhausted all means of making a living. Such as I am, I will get a lot of money from her in this way, with very little trouble.' Or, 'This woman is madly in love

> with me and knows all my weaknesses. If I reject her, she will ruin me by publicly exposing my faults; or she will accuse me of some fault which I do not in fact have, but which will be easy to believe of me and hard to clear myself of, and this will be the ruin of me.'[25]

This is a brilliant and timeless portrait of a self-serving rascal who has no illusions about himself.

THE POSITIONS

Our reaction to the central subject, the act of love, should surely be one of recognition, of familiarity, but no. Here, rather than in the cultural setting, is where we are, unexpectedly, brought up short by the unfamiliar. But the passage describing the ways that a man can move inside a woman seem to cut right through culture to human nature—until we are once again brought up sharp by the quaint names that are given to these movements (and that have been a subject of parody ever since Sir Richard Burton's translation became widely known in the English-speaking world, after 1883):

> When he reams her many times just on one side, that is the 'boar's thrust'. When he does this to both sides, alternating, it is the 'bull's thrust'. When he enters her once and, without pulling out entirely, thrusts into her two, three, four times, and does this repeatedly, it is called 'frolicking like a sparrow'.[26]

The *Kamasutra* describes a number of contortions that 'require practice', as the text puts it mildly, and these are the positions that generally make people laugh, uneasily, at the mention of the *Kamasutra*.

Vatsyayana attributes some of the more difficult positions to his rival Suvarnanabha:

> Now for those of Suvarnanabha: When both thighs of the woman are raised, it is called the 'curve'. When the man holds her legs up, it is the 'yawn'. When he does that but also flexes her legs at the knees, it is the 'high-squeeze'. When he does that but stretches out one of her feet, it is the 'half-squeeze'. When one of her feet is placed on the man's shoulder and the other is stretched out, and they alternate again and again, this is called 'splitting the bamboo'. When one of her legs is raised above her head and the other leg is stretched out, it is called 'impaling on a stake', and can only be done with practice. When both of her legs are flexed at the knees and placed on her own abdomen, it is the 'crab'. When her thighs are raised and crossed, it is the 'squeeze'. When she opens her knees and crosses her calves, it is the 'lotus seat'. When he turns around with his back to her, and she embraces his back, that is called 'rotating', and can only be done with practice.[27]

Evidently, Vatsyayana regards these as over the top, which is why he blames them on someone else, Suvarnanabha.

What are we to make of these gymnastics? Did people in ancient India really make love like that? I think not. True, they did have yoga, and great practitioners of yoga can make their bodies do things that most other people would not think possible (or even, perhaps, desirable). But just because one can do it is no reason that one *should* do it. (Or, as Vatsyayana remarks, first at the end of his passage about oral sex and same-sex sex,[28] and again at the end of his Viagra passage,[29] 'The statement that "There is a text for this" does not justify a practice.' This is actually the only verse that he repeats in the whole book; it is important to him.)

But I think the answer lies elsewhere:

> Vatsyayana says: Even passion demands variety. And it is through variety that partners inspire passion in one another. It is their infinite variety that makes courtesans and their lovers remain desirable to one another. Even in archery and in other martial arts, the textbooks insist on variety. How much more is this true of sex![30]

The extreme positions may simply be the artiste's free-ranging fantasies on a theme of sexual possibilities: they are not instructive but inspiring, and inspired. The text is a virtual sexual *pas de deux* as Georges Balanchine might have choreographed it, an extended meditation on some of the ways that a naked man and a naked woman (or, rarely, several men and/or women) might move their limbs while making love. It represents a literally no-holds-barred exploration of the theoretical possibilities of human heterosexual coupling, much as the profusion of fantastical compound animals in other texts—heads of horses on the bodies of women, or torsos of women on the bodies of cobras, and so forth—push back the walls of our imagination of the variety of known and unknown animal species. It is a fantasy literature, an artistic and imaginative, rather than physical, exploration of coupling. And it boggles the contemporary imagination.

Though sexual reality may in fact be universal—there are, after all, just so many things that you can do with your genitals—sexual fantasy seems to be highly cultural. This, then, is what is new to us in the brave new world of this ancient text, in which the constant alternation of the familiar and the strange teaches us a great deal about human nature and human culture.

# 2

# THE KAUTILYAN *KAMASUTRA*

## THE TRIPLE SET OF HUMAN AIMS

Yashodhara, the thirteenth century commentator on the *Kamasutra,* told the following story at the very start of his commentary:

> The three aims of human life are three divinities...And there is textual evidence that they are in fact divinities. For the historian tells us: 'When King Pururavas went from earth to heaven to see Indra, the king of the gods, he saw Dharma (Religion), Artha (Power) and Kama (Pleasure) embodied. As he approached them, he ignored the other two but paid homage to Dharma, walking around him in a circle to the right. The other two, unable to put up with this slight, cursed him. Because Kama had cursed him, he was separated from his wife, Urvashi, and longed for her in her absence. When he had managed to put that right, then, because Artha had cursed him, he became so excessively greedy that he stole from all four social classes. The Brahmins, who were upset because they could no longer perform the sacrifice or other rituals without the money he had stolen from them, took blades of sharp sacrificial grass in their hands and killed him.[1]

There is a parallel to this story in the Greek myth of Paris, who, forced to choose between three goddesses, chose Aphrodite (= Kama) over Hera and Athene (roughly = Dharma and Artha), who cursed him.[2] The Indian commentator refers elsewhere, briefly, to a different variant of the Indian version of the myth when he remarks that Artha, when it overrides all else, impedes dharma and kama (as it did for Pururavas).[3] Indeed, the story tells us how compelling and dangerous artha and kama can be, but also how dharma, especially when invoked by Brahmins, is the most powerful of all. (It also tells us that Brahmins are capable of violently defending their right to be paid for performing rituals.) Not everyone, however, believed this story, or the assumptions that underlie it. Many people—who included, I will argue, the authors of the oldest texts of the sciences of artha and kama—did not swallow the myth at all.

Ancient Hindu texts often speak of dharma, artha and kama as the three aims of human life (or *purusharthas*, also called the *trivarga*, or the Triple Set), which every person was supposed to achieve in order to have a full life. For assonance, one might call them piety, profit, and pleasure, or society, success, and sex, or duty, domination, and desire. More precisely, dharma includes duty, religion, religious merit, morality, social obligations, justice, righteousness and the law—the good life. Artha is money, political power, profit, and success—the high life.[4] Kama represents love, desire, and pleasure (what the Germans call *Wollust* and *Lust*), not merely sexual but more broadly sensual—music, good food, perfume—the fine life. (During this same period, some people began to speak of a Quadruple Set [*chaturvarga*], with a fourth aim of *moksha* or Release from the eternal cycle of rebirths. But *moksha* will not concern us much in our present discussion, for the *Arthashastra* and *Kamasutra* speak only of a Triple Set.)

Each of the three aims is the subject of a science or

discipline (*shastra*), embodied in any number of texts, and these texts, composed in Sanskrit, are also (rather confusingly) called *shastras*. So Ashva-shastra in general means the science of horse-breeding and –training (*ashva* corresponds to the Latin *equus*), while the *Ashvashastra* attributed to a particular author is a textbook about horse-breeding and-training.

In the science of dharma, the *Dharmashastra* attributed to Manu is the most famous; it is cited in other ancient Indian texts far more frequently than any other *dharmashastra*. The *Arthashastra* attributed to Kautilya is similarly outstanding for artha; it is a compendium of advice for a king, combining much technical information on the running of a kingdom with a good deal of thought on the subject of human psychology. Together with the *Kamasutra,* these two texts form a triad that will supply the main substance of this chapter. Manu will serve us primarily as a baseline from which the other two texts diverge.

## THE HISTORY OF THE THREE TEXTS, AND THEIR INTERTEXTUALITY

The history of the three texts is a tangled labyrinth of mutual influences. It begins with the *Arthashastra*, which is generally attributed to Kautilya ("Crookedness"[5]), also called Chanakya and Vishnugupta, the brilliant minister who helped the Mauryan emperor Chandragupta to win and maintain a great empire, beginning in the fourth century BCE. And indeed, there may have been some sort of rudimentary *Arthashastra* at the time of the Mauryas. But the actual text of our *Arthashastra* first began to be compiled in the middle of the first century CE, when someone who called himself Kautilya composed the text as a guide for a king (and his principal advisors and ministers) in the management of economic and military affairs.

Then, sometime in the second half of the second century CE, someone who called himself Manu composed a major *Dharmashastra*. This was neither the first not the last of this genre, but it was the first to incorporate discussions of governance, royal duties, and law, subjects that actually take up more than a third of the text. For these subjects, Manu borrowed heavily from Kautilya. And then, sometime after the second century CE, another scholar updated Kautilya's text by adding material from Manu and other *dharmashastras*. This is the *Arthashastra* text that we have, a palimpsest starting from a now lost *Arthashastra*, which fed into a *Dharmashastra* by Manu, which fed, in turn, into an *Arthashastra* that incorporated elements from Manu.

The *Arthashastra* is about a century older than the *Kamasutra* and gives no evidence of knowledge of any *Kamasutra*, nor does it mention kama as an organizing system. The *Kamasutra* mentions an *Arthashastra* explicitly once[6] (and implicitly elsewhere) but not necessarily Kautilya's: it draws primarily on the portions of the *Arthashastra* that concern merchants making money and the superintendents of commerce and agriculture,[7] not the guide for kings.[8]

So the first version of the *Arthashastra* came first (middle of the first century CE); Manu (second half of the second century CE) borrowed from that version of the *Arthashastra* and then in turn influenced the second recension of the *Arthashastra* (early third century CE); and that compendium of *Arthashastra* and Manu influenced the (late third century

CE) *Kamasutra*. The *Arthashastra* and Manu quote one another, and the *Kamasutra* quotes the *Arthashastra*. They are all in conversation, intertextuality with a vengeance. Though they differ spectacularly on a number of ethical issues, these texts exist together in one world; the differences between them are not only the differences caused by shifts in context of time and place; more important are the differences between different sorts of people, in different parts of the same society at the same time. It is not the case that only a puritanical Brahmin studied the dharma texts and only a libertine merchant read the *Kamasutra*; no, the same man, of either class, might well read dharma with learned men (pandits) by day and the *Kamasutra* with his mistress by night.

## THE INDEBTEDNESS OF THE *KAMASUTRA* TO THE *ARTHASHASTRA*

We've seen that the author of the revised standard edition of the *Arthashastra* borrowed heavily from Manu (and vice versa). It should therefore not be surprising to learn that the *Kamasutra* borrowed heavily from the *Arthashastra* (though, in this case, the *Arthashastra* did not return the compliment). While the *Arthashastra* is deeply suspicious of kama in any shape or form, the *Kamasutra* has respect for artha as an aim, especially as far as courtesans are concerned. The *Kamasutra* is closely based upon the *Arthashastra*, and this connection strongly influences the worldview of the *Kamasutra*. The *Panchatantra*, the book of beast fables, is in many ways a spoof on the *Arthashastra*; the *Kamasutra* is in many ways a variation on selected themes of the *Arthashastra*.

Other scholars have noticed the influence of the *form* of the *Arthashastra* on the *Kamasutra*, but haven't realized how extensively and closely the *content* and *philosophy* of the *Kamasutra* are constrained by those of the *Arthashastra*. I will explore first the evidence for this influence and then the ways in which the *Kamasutra* pulls away from the *Arthashastra*. I'll conclude with a brief speculation about the way that the *Kamasutra* applies to sex the principles of politics, more precisely the shamelessly unethical politics of the *Arthashastra,* and the implications of this connection for the later history of erotic and religious literature in India.

## BASIC SIMILARITIES OF FORM AND ARGUMENT

The *Arthashastra* and *Kamasutra* are alike in a number of ways, as we will soon see, but perhaps the most basic is the cluster of ways in which they both differ from Manu. This is immediately apparent from their form: Manu is in verse throughout, the same simple *shloka* metre as that of the two great Sanskrit epics, the *Ramayana* and the *Mahabharata*, while the *Arthashastra* and *Kamasutra* are in prose, usually capped with a verse or two at the end of a chapter. The *Kamasutra* models both its format and its rhetoric closely on that of the *Arthashastra*. Prose chapters, containing down-to-earth, often non-dharmic or even anti-dharmic instructions, are capped by verses that express often contradictory, generally dharmic exhortations. This hypocritical attitude to religion, as well as the use of verses to express the pro-dharmic overlay, is another trait that the two texts have in common.

More significant perhaps is the pattern of the three texts'

ways of arguing. Manu never actually argues at all: like a parent to a child, he presents primarily 'because' statements (explicit dogmas or appeals to authority: do it because I say so) and, only occasionally, 'this is why' arguments (implicit rationalizations or appeals to persuasion). He also sometimes simply juxtaposes conflicting views, without prioritizing them or making any attempt to reconcile them.

In the *Arthashastra* and *Kamasutra*, by contrast, there are genuine arguments: a point of view is stated and defended, an opposing view stated, sometimes a series of views, and the author caps it with what he regards as the best argument. Such argument is generally characteristic of the scientific shastras; the medical textbooks, for instance, depict a series of physicians arguing about the etiology of a disease until the author states his own view.[9] And the *Arthashastra* and *Kamasutra* put this tradition to work in the tap dance they do around dharma.

## ATTITUDES TO LOW-LIFE AND KINGS

Another sharp difference between Manu, on the one hand, and the *Arthashastra* and the *Kamasutra*, on the other, can be seen in their attitudes to what ancient India regarded as marginalized people: Manu tells you to avoid them at all costs, while the *Arthashastra* and *Kamasutra* tell you to use them, as spies (*Arthashastra*) or go-betweens (*Kamasutra*). To consider just one list among many such, Manu warns you not to eat the food which someone has sneezed on (which makes good sense), but then he continues, 'nor the food of a slanderer, a liar, or the seller of rituals, nor the food of a tumbler or a weaver, nor the food of an ingrate; nor that of a blacksmith, a strolling actor, a goldsmith, a basket-weaver, or an arms-dealer; nor that of a man who raises dogs, a bootlegger, a washerman, or a dyer'.[10] Manu cites a similar list in another context, of those who will end up in the lowest forms of rebirth: strolling actors, pugilists, wrestlers, dancers, arms-dealers, and addicted gamblers and drunks.[11] He also remarks that the rules against speaking with women do not apply to the wives of strolling actors or of men who live off their own wives; for these men have their women embrace other men, concealing themselves while they have them do the act; nor is there any serious punishment for a man who carries on a conversation secretly with these women, or with menial servant girls who are used by only one man, or with wandering women ascetics.[12] Manu's dislike of actors—indeed of all artistes—stems in part from their ability to make the unreal seem real.[13] But such people—as well as the wandering women ascetics—are an essential part of Vatsyayana's crew of panders, libertines, and clowns, while actors and musicians are also Kautilya's basic CIA material, as when, for instance, the king wishes to liberate a prince held hostage:

> Actors, dancers, singers, musicians, bards, performers, rope-dancers, and dramatic storytellers, who had been infiltrated beforehand, should wait upon the enemy. They should wait upon the prince one after another, and he should dictate that they may enter, stay, and exit without time restrictions. Then he should go away at night disguised as one of them. This also explains courtesans and women disguised as wives. Or else, he should get out carrying the packages of their musical instruments.[14]

Religious mendicants and ascetics, both male and female, are always a part of this marginal society. Manu tells you how to be an ascetic;[15] Kautilya tells a spy to pretend to be an ascetic; and Vatsyayana tells you to employ an ascetic as a go-between.[16] It's a three-way conversation, as the three texts are manipulating the same cultural conventions in different ways.

## ATTITUDES TO OTHER SCHOLARS

Both Vatsyayana and Kautilya begin with invocations, followed by an acknowledgement of their debt to previous texts on their respective subjects. (We do not have these texts, but both the anthological nature of our two texts and their explicit statement of indebtedness to other texts strongly suggest that such texts existed.) Thus the *Arthashastra* states:

> This [singular *Arthashastra*] has been composed for the most part by drawing together the *Arthashastras* composed by former teachers for gaining and administering the earth.[17]

Vatsyayana, too, begins by invoking his academic ancestors[18] and continues in a long paragraph[19] that mentions the predecessors by name.[20] The *Arthashastra* does not name Kautilya's predecessors in its initial invocation, but it does name them elsewhere, as, for instance, in the long argument about whether or not the king should kill his sons as soon as they are born,[21] and in another argument about the people who are eligible to be ministers of state.[22] Correspondingly, the *Kamasutra* invokes its authorities, one by one, in an argument about what sorts of women are and are not eligible as sexual partners.[23]

## STRIKING POINTS OF AGREEMENT

Within this shared framework there are also a number of incidental passages in which the *Arthashastra* has clearly provided the paradigm for the *Kamasutra*. For example, the *Arthashastra* gives elaborate instructions on setting up the royal residence:

> On land recommended as a building site, he should get a royal residence constructed with palisade, moat, and gates, and provided with many courtyards...In an area of the courtyard at the back should be the women's quarters, maternity room, infirmary, and a yard with trees and water. Outside is the residence for young girls and princes. In the front are the dressing room, the counsel chamber, the assembly hall, and the offices for the supervisors of the princes. In the areas between the courtyards should be stationed the palace guard.[24]

And, on a more intimate scale, this is how, *mutatis mutandis*, the *Kamasutra* instructs the man-about-town to set up his pad:

> He makes his home in a house near water, with an orchard, separate servant quarters, and two bedrooms. This is how the house is furnished: In the outer bedroom there is a bed, low in the middle and very soft, with pillows on both sides and a white top sheet. (There is also a couch.) At the head of the bed there is a grass mat and an altar, on which are placed the oils and garlands left over from the night, a pot of bees' wax, a vial of perfume, some bark from a lemon tree, and betel. On the floor, a spitoon. A lute, hanging from an ivory tusk; a board to draw or paint on, and a box of pencils. Some book or other, and garlands of amaranth

> flowers. On the floor, not too far away, a round bed with a pillow for the head. A board for dice and a board for gambling. Outside, cages of pet birds. And, set aside, a place for carpentry or woodworking and for other games. In the orchard, a well-padded swing in the shade, and a bench made of baked clay and covered with flowers.[25]

The *Kamasutra* goes into much more detail about the layout of the bedroom, of course,[i] and lacks the detailed description of fortifications that the *Arthashastra* supplies, but the blueprints take the same form in both cases.

The *Arthashastra* advises the king to make use of actors dressed as gods of fire and water, to demoralize the enemy during a siege.[26] The *Kamasutra* prescribes similar play-acting to a man laying siege, as it were, to a virgin: he should have a friend dress up not as a god but as a fortune-teller and describe the 'man's future good luck and prosperity' to the girl's mother to earn her favour.[27] The use of black magic is strikingly similar in the two texts, both of which discuss it at length at the end of the text, as a kind of afterthought or last resort. (And both touch on magic in passing in other parts of the text, the *Kamasutra* only a few times, the *Arthashastra* a great deal). The *Arthashastra* permits a man to use love-magic on a disaffected wife or a wife to use it on her husband,[28] while the *Kamasutra* cautions wives not to use it on adulterous husbands;[29] but, on the other hand, Vatsyayana devotes an entire book (Book Seven) to the magic that a man can use on women, while the corresponding book of the *Arthashastra* (Book Fourteen) is devoted to magic used for various purposes, mostly murder, but never love. Still

i See chapter six, 'The Mare's Trap'.

the magic techniques overlap in interesting ways. Both the *Arthashastra*[30] and the *Kamasutra*[31] offer magic spells to make you invisible, using an ointment that you put on *your* eyes, projecting sightlessness onto the person who looks at you. Both texts are concerned that, when you make yourself invisible, your shadow, too, must be invisible.[32] (The *Arthashastra*, but not the *Kamasutra*, says that you should burn the ingredients for this ointment in a woman's vagina.) And both texts offer formulas for magic to make you white, the purpose of which is unclear (to me) in both cases.[33]

## SPYING

The paranoid psychology of the political text casts its shadow over the erotic text. Though the *Arthashastra* is often said to be Machiavellian (the standard Sanskrit dictionary of Sir Monier Monier-Williams refers to Kautilya/Chanakya as 'the Machiavelli of India'), Kautilya makes Machiavelli look like Mother Teresa. Suspicion, treachery, and trickery pervade the *Arthashastra*, and much of this carries over into the *Kamasutra*.

The *Arthashastra* list of people in the enemy's territory who are dissatisfied and can therefore be seduced politically is the model for the *Kamasutra* list of women in their husband's territory, as it were, who are dissatisfied, or unsatisfied, and so can be seduced sexually.

First the *Arthashastra*:

> We have explained how seducible and non-seducible factions may be won over within one's own territory; we have yet to describe how it is carried out in an enemy's territory.

The set of angry people is as follows: someone who is cheated out of things he had been promised; between two people who carry out a craft or a service equally well, the one who is slighted; someone disgraced on account of a king's favourite; someone who is defeated after being challenged; someone who is incensed at being exiled; someone who did not get the job after incurring expenses; someone who is prevented from carrying out the Law specific to him or from receiving his inheritance; someone stripped of honours or office; someone held back by members of the royal family; someone whose wife has been forcibly molested; someone put in prison; someone who has been fined after losing a lawsuit; someone who has been restrained from engaging in wrongful conduct; someone whose entire property has been confiscated; someone who has been harassed in prison; and someone whose relative has been executed.

The set of frightened people is as follows: someone who has hurt another; someone who has committed a wrong; someone whose sinful acts have been disclosed; someone who is alarmed at a punishment meted out for a similar crime; someone who has seized land; someone who has surrendered with his troops; a head of any department who has suddenly become wealthy; someone who expects a pretender from the royal family to succeed; someone detested by the king; and someone who hates the king.

The set of greedy people is as follows: someone who has become destitute; someone whose property has been taken by another; a miser; someone who has fallen on hard times; and someone who has entered into ill-considered business transactions.

The set of proud people is as follows: someone who thinks highly of himself; someone desirous of honours;

> someone rankled by the respect paid to an enemy; someone who has been demoted; someone with a bad temper; someone who is violent; and someone dissatisfied with his compensation.
>
> Among these, he should incite to sedition each individual belonging to a seducible faction through one of the agents working undercover as shaven-headed or matted-hair ascetics to whom he may be devoted.[34]

The *Kamasutra* apes this technique:

> Just as a man judges his chances of success from considering his own qualities, so he should judge them from considering the woman's qualities, too. The following are women who can be had without any effort, who can be had merely by making advances: a woman who stands at the door; a woman who looks out from her rooftop-porch onto the main street; a woman who hangs about the house of the young man who is her neighbour; a woman who stares constantly; a woman who, when someone looks at her, looks sideways; a woman who has been supplanted by a co-wife for no cause; a woman who hates her husband; a woman who is hated; a woman who lacks restraint; a woman who has no children; a woman who has always lived in the house of her relatives; a woman whose children have died; a woman who is fond of society; a woman who shows her love; the wife of an actor; a young woman whose husband has died; a poor woman fond of enjoying herself; the wife of the oldest of several brothers; a very proud woman who has an inadequate husband; a woman who is proud of her skills and distressed by her husband's foolishness, lack of distinction, or greediness; a woman who, when she was a virgin, was courted by a man who made a great effort but somehow did not get her and now

> woos her again; a woman whose intelligence, nature, wisdom, perception, and personality are similar to those of the would-be lover; a woman who is by nature given to taking sides; a woman who has been dishonoured by her husband when she has done nothing wrong; a woman who is put down by women whose beauty and so forth are the same as hers; a woman whose husband travels a lot; the wife of a man who is jealous, putrid, too pure, impotent, a procrastinator, unmanly, a hunchback, a dwarf, deformed, a jeweller, a villager, bad-smelling, sick, or old.[35]

In a similar parallelism, the internal debate of potential adulterers, in the *Kamasutra,* persuading themselves of the moral justice of their actions,[36] mirrors the similarly imagined meditations of spies in the *Arthashastra*[37] and the king's self-persuasions and justifications for seizing power.[38]

Another trait that the *Kamasutra* clearly picks up from the *Arthashastra* is the constant use of male and female messengers (*dutas*), which makes little sense in the *Kamasutra* except as a replication of the far more meaningful constant employment of male and female spies (*dutas* again) in the *Arthashastra.*[39] Both texts recommend the use of monks, nuns, and religious mendicants as spies (*Arthashastra*) or go-betweens (*Kamasutra*), in neither case demonstrating the least bit of respect for the possible actual religiosity, or reputation, of such people. Both texts pay close attention to peoples' involuntary gestures and revealing facial expressions as betrayals of hidden political or, as the case may be, sexual emotions. (This art was also developed in the textbook of acting and dancing, the *Natyashastra*, composed during this same general period.) All of this spying casts a presumption of dishonesty and betrayal over erotic relationships, a mood that remains a part of Hindu erotic discourse.

The *Arthashastra* notes the particular character flaw of each official that causes each particular problem:

> An official may cause a loss of revenue—through ignorance, if he is unacquainted with the procedures, customs, and canons; through laziness, if he is incapable of enduring the travails of entrepreneurial activity; through carelessness, if he is addicted to sensual objects such as sound; through fear, if he is scared of agitations or of acting against dharma or artha; through kama, if he is inclined to favour those who come to plead their cases, and through anger, if he is inclined to hurt them; through arrogance, if he relies on his learning, wealth, or connection to a royal favourite; and through greed, if he inserts discrepancies in weights, measures, estimates, and accounting.[40]

The *Kamasutra* cleverly adapts this template into a precise and rather cunning psychology for devising approaches to women who are differently resistant to adultery, tailoring each approach to the particular source of resistance[41]:

> A man should eliminate, from the very beginning, whichever of these causes for rejection he detects in his own situation. If it is connected with her nobility, he excites more passion. If it is a matter of apparent impossibility, he shows her ways to manage it. If the problem is her respect for him, he becomes very intimate with her. If it stems from her contempt, he demonstrates his extraordinary pride and his erudition. If it comes from his contempt, he prostrates himself before her. If she is afraid, he reassures her.[42]

In yet another pair of closely parallel texts, the *Arthashastra* presents a four-fold typology of repentant traitors:

> Those who have left and returned are of four types: one who left and returned for a proper reason, and the opposite of this; one who left for a proper reason but returned without a proper reason, and the opposite of that.[43]

It is but the work of a moment for the *Kamasutra* to convert this into a six-fold typology of lovers who leave the courtesan and then may or may not be taken back:

> If he has gone elsewhere, she must find out about him; he may belong in any of the six possible categories, according to the circumstances: He left her of his own accord and he left the other woman, too, of his own accord. He left both her and the other woman because they got rid of him. He left her of his own accord and he left the other woman because she got rid of him. He left her of his own accord and stayed with the other woman. He left her because she got rid of him and he left the other woman of his own accord. He left her because she got rid of him and he stayed with the other woman. [44]

## TESTING

The influence of the *Arthashastra* on the *Kamasutra* is particularly visible in the techniques of testing. With the concern for particular individuals that we have noted as a property of effective spying, the *Arthashastra* suggests various ways to deal with young princes variously susceptible to hunting, gambling, liquor, and women (which the *Kamasutra*, too, echoing Manu, defines elsewhere as the four royal vices or the vices that spring from lust [45]). First, Kautilya objects to the suggestion that the crown prince be tempted:

> One of the secret agents, moreover, should entice him with hunting, gambling, liquor, and women, saying, 'Attack your father and seize the kingdom.' Another secret agent should dissuade him…Says Kautilya, 'To awaken one who is not awake is greatly detrimental, for a fresh object absorbs anything smeared on it. In like manner, a prince, whose mind is fresh, will accept anything he is told as if it were the teaching of a *shastra*. Therefore, one should teach him what accords with dharma and artha, never anything that is contrary to dharma and artha.[46]

Instead, Kautilya suggests that the prince be subjected to a kind of aversion therapy:

> The secret agents…should guard [the prince], saying, 'We are yours.' If he sets his mind on other people's wives out of youthful insolence, they should make him recoil by introducing him at night in deserted houses to squalid women posing as noble ladies. If he takes a fancy for liquor, they should make him recoil by administering a doctored drink. If he takes a fancy for gambling, they should make him recoil with the help of crafty-student agents. If he takes a fancy for hunting, they should frighten him through agents posing as bandits.[47]

More specifically, however, the *Arthashastra* advises the king to test his potential ministers of various departments to make sure they are impervious to the temptations of each of the three aims of life, able to say 'No' to dharma, artha or kama. He also tells him to test the candidate against a fourth aim, not *moksha* but fear (often listed as the fourth emotion, after the primary triad of desire, anger, and greed).[48] The third test, the test of kama, in the *Arthashastra* is this:

> A female wandering ascetic who has won the confidence of and is received with honour in the royal residence should instigate each high official individually: 'The chief queen is in love with you and has made arrangements to meet with you. You will also receive a lot of money.' If he rebuffs it, he is a man of integrity. That is the secret test relating to kama.[49]

And any man who has thus been proven impervious to kama is to be made a guard of the harem.[50] Those who successfully resist dharma are to be put in charge of the courts, or, for resisting the temptation of artha, the treasury. Those who have proved that they have no fear may qualify as royal bodyguards.

This programme then appears in the *Kamasutra* as just a single test for the guards of the harem, but this one test combines the four elements, including fear, that the *Arthashastra* used to test four different sorts of ministers:

> Scholars say: 'Guards stationed in the harem should be proved pure by the trial of kama.' Gonikaputra says: 'But fear or artha may make them let the women use another man; therefore guards should be proved pure by the trials of kama, fear and artha.' Vatsyayana says: 'Dharma prevents treachery. But a man will abandon even dharma because of fear. Therefore guards should be proved pure by the trial of dharma and fear.'[51]

In the end, therefore, and in contradiction of Kautilya (whose opinion Vatsyayana cites under the rubric of 'scholars'), Vatsyayana decides that imperviousness to kama is not the most important quality for a harem guard, after all; fear and dharma trump kama. But since the *Arthashastra* precedes the *Kamasutra* logically as well as chronologically, when the *Kamasutra* tries to adopt the *Arthashastra* scheme for testing ministers to a scheme for testing the guards in the harem, it has to condense it so that each guard is tested in four ways, some of which are totally irrelevant to the qualities of a guard in the harem.

Kautilya, by contrast, states that the men who guard the harem need not be tested for kama, since they should be 'at least eighty years old', fatherly, or elderly celibate stewards.[52] On the other hand, again unlike Vatsyayana, he suggests that the *women* of the harem must themselves be tested for 'honesty and dishonesty', lest they prove a danger to the king. For Kautilya is primarily concerned not so much to protect the king's wives (Vatsyayana's concern) as to protect the king *from* his wives:[53]

> Going to the inner chamber, he should meet with the queen after she has been inspected and cleared by elderly women. For Bhadrasena was killed by his brother hiding in the queen's chamber, and Karusha by his son hiding under his mother's bed. The king of Kashi was killed by his queen with puffed grain mixed with poison disguised as honey; Vairantya with an anklet smeared with poison; Sauvira with a girdle-jewel smeared with poison; and Jalutha with a mirror smeared with poison. And the queen killed Viduratha by hiding a weapon in her braids. Therefore, he should avoid these situations.[54]

There is no direct parallel to this list in the *Kamasutra*, which never warns men about physical dangers from women but often warns them against the physical harm that they may cause women. But, as we are about to see below, the *form* of the warning—the list of mythical and historical characters who were destroyed by kama—does indeed appear in both texts to make the same related point: the danger to men posed by their own kama, usually in the form of attacks by the men whom they have cuckolded.

And there is another close parallel that appears in the context of this testing. The *Arthashastra*, speaking of testing the ministers, warns against the danger that one might corrupt the uncorrupted, 'like water with poison; for it may well be that a remedy may not be found for a person who has been corrupted'.[55] So, too, when other 'scholars'[56] suggest that the young prince be tested by tempting him to attack his father and seize the kingdom, Kautilya objects, as we have noted earlier in the chapter: 'To awaken one who is not awake is greatly detrimental, for a fresh object absorbs anything smeared on it…'

This same concern appears when the *Kamasutra* speaks of testing the chastity of wives:

> The followers of Babhravya say: 'To find out about his own wives' purity or impurity, a man should test them through charming women who have deeply hidden their own involuntary signals and who will report what other people say.' But Vatsyayana says: Because corrupt people can succeed among young women, a man should not set in motion, without a reason, the corruption of a person who is not corrupt.[57]

And so the *Kamasutra* suggests better ways to control women, primarily through knowledge of the *Kamasutra*.

## THE NEED TO CONTROL THE SENSES

Manu, as you might expect, has a very long section warning the king about self-control.[58] Turning to the other two texts, one would have thought that the concern for the control of the senses would make far more sense in the *Arthashastra* context than in the *Kamasutra*, but not so. An emphasis on the need for a man to control not (or not just) his women but his own senses pervades both texts. As Lorraine Daston sharply summarizes the issue, 'Since both artha and (surprisingly for Western readers) kama depend on control, on the postponed gratification that scheming demands, there is after all a natural link with dharma: the person capable of far-sighted calculation, sacrifice of short-term indulgence of the passions for long-term gain, and understanding of how individuals interact (and therefore how they can be manipulated) is also the person with sufficient self-discipline and social savvy to practise dharma.'[59]

The *Arthashastra* sees as more dangerous than any other threat the enemy within, more precisely the 'six enemies' within: desire, anger, and greed—the original triad of emotions—plus pride, conceit, and excitement:

> Mastery over the senses results from training in the knowledge systems and is to be accomplished by giving up desire, anger, greed, pride, conceit, and excitement...This entire treatise boils down to the mastery over the senses. A king who behaves contrary to it and has no control over his senses will perish immediately, even though he may rule the four ends of the earth. [60]

Again and again, the *Arthashastra* speaks of the need for control: '[He] should gain mastery over the senses by abandoning the set of six enemies.'[61] Spies, in particular, are advised to avoid women and liquor, to stay sober and sleep alone,[62] for people reveal secrets through the indiscretions of love affairs.[63]

The *Arthashastra*'s list of kings (Bhadrasena *et al*) who were destroyed by treacherous women (with mirrors or lips smeared with poison and so forth) is matched by another *Arthashastra* list of kings who were destroyed by the far more dangerous enemies within:

> The Bhoja king named Dandakya, for example, who violated the young daughter of a Brahmin through desire, was destroyed along with his kinsmen and kingdom; so also Karala of Videha; Janamejaya assailing Brahmins out of anger, as also Talajangha assailing the Bhrigus; Aila extorting money from the four social classes out of greed, as also Ajabindu of the Sauviras; Ravana not returning the wife of another out of pride, as also Duryodhana not returning a portion of the kingdom; Dambhodbhava treating people with contempt out of conceit, as also Arjuna of the Haihayas; Vatapi assailing Agastya through excitement, as also the Vrishni confederacy assailing Dvaipayana. These and many other kings, addicted to the set of six enemies and not having mastered their senses, came to ruin along with their kinsmen and kingdoms. Having abandoned the set of six enemies, Jamadagnya, who had mastered his senses, as well as Ambarisha, the son of Nabhaga, enjoyed the earth for a long time.[64]

The *Kamasutra* uses an abbreviated version of the very same list, beginning with a word-for-word quotation of the tale of the first unfortunate sinner on the *Arthashastra* list, Dandakya:[ii]

> For instance, when the Bhoja king named Dandakya was aroused by a Brahmin's daughter, desire destroyed him,

---

ii For more about Dandakya, see chapter three, 'The Mythology of the *Kamasutra*'.

> along with his relatives and his kingdom. And Indra the king of the gods with Ahalya, the super-powerful Kichaka with Draupadi, Ravana with Sita, and many others afterwards were seen to fall into the thrall of desire and were destroyed.[65]

(Ravana, the villain of the *Ramayana,*[iii] appears on both lists.) But Vatsyayana in this passage is not speaking for himself; he is quoting 'people who worry too much about artha' [*arthachintakas*], people we might call Pragmatists, but in any case people of 'other schools' whom Vatsyayana imagines as objecting to his book about kama. (He answers these objections by pointing out that, despite its dangers, kama is as necessary to human beings as food is.[66]) But is Vatsyayana just imagining such people? Is it not more likely that here he is actually quoting the *Arthashastra*, and obliquely criticizing Kautilya for worrying too much about artha? Certainly Kautilya's definition of the shortcomings of kama—'Kama involves disgrace, the depletion of resources and association with undesirable people: robbers, gamblers, hunters, singers, and musicians'[67]—seems to be precisely what Vatsyayana quotes the 'people who worry about artha' as saying (an opinion to which he strenuously objects): 'Kama makes a man associate with worthless people and undertake bad projects, [and makes him] impure, a man with no future, as well as careless, lightweight, untrustworthy and unacceptable.'[68] And though the *Kamasutra* remarks that a king 'who suppresses the band of six enemies within him conquers the earth too',[69] this sentiment occurs in a verse at the end of a chapter, where Vatsyayana usually

iii See chapter three, 'The Mythology of the *Kamasutra*'.

lodges pious sayings that he has contradicted at numerous points of the preceding chapter.

Elsewhere, Vatsyayana cites, with agreement, some anonymous sage (Kautilya?) voicing other, similar warnings, not about kama in general but about certain forms of it that are politically dangerous:

> The man in power should not enter another man's home [to take his wife]. 'For when Abhira, the Kotta king, went to another man's home, a washerman employed by the king's brother killed him. And the superintendant of horses killed Jayasena the king of Varanasi.' So it is said.[70]

Since neither Abhira nor Jayasena appears in the extant *Arthashastra*, literal citation of Kautilya is unlikely, but the *form* is Kautilyan, and Kautilya may in fact be the person Vatsyayana has in mind when he remarks, 'So it is said.'

The *Kamasutra* also uses the formulaic citation of mythical tales of people who died in sexual situations to warn men about the harm that they may do to women:

> One should also avoid, even in the region where it is used, anything that is dangerous. The King of the Cholas killed Chitrasena, a courtesan de luxe, by using the 'wedge' during sex. And the Kuntala king Shatakarni Shatavahana killed his queen, Malayavati, by using the 'scissor'. Naradeva, whose hand was deformed, blinded a dancing girl in one eye by using the 'drill' clumsily.[71]

The *Arthashastra*, by contrast, cannot apparently even imagine this sort of injury.

## THE *ARTHASHASTRA* AND *KAMASUTRA* ON SEX

This brings us to our final concern, the area in which the texts most explicitly converge, which is in the treatment of sexuality; for though the *Kamasutra* has, as we have seen, absorbed a great many political attitudes from the *Arthashastra*, it seldom discusses politics explicitly, while the *Arthashastra* does explicitly address sexual issues at various points. (Manu does not provide a very useful benchmark here, since all he has to say about sex is to forbid sodomy and bestiality and to advise the reader not to eat the food of 'a man whose wife's lover lives in his house; nor that of those who put up with such lovers, or who are dominated by their wives in all things'.[72]) But the *Arthashastra* and *Kamasutra* agree on some points about sexuality and disagree on others. Let us begin with the agreements.

In the *Arthashastra*, sex is merely the background for political power, whereas, in the *Kamasutra*, political power is merely the background for sex. But the *Kamasutra*'s list of reasons that justify adultery include many that are far more political than erotic. This is some of what the would-be adulterer says to himself:

> 'This woman has her husband entirely under her control, and he is a great and powerful man who is intimate with my enemy. If she becomes intimate with me, out of her affection for me she will make him reverse his allegiance.' Or, 'That powerful man has turned against me and wishes to harm me; she will bring him back to his former nature.' Or, 'If I make him my friend through her, I will be able to do favours for my friends, or ward off my enemies, or accomplish some other difficult undertaking.' Or, 'If I become intimate with this woman, and kill her husband, I

> will get for myself the power of his great wealth, which ought to be mine.' Or…'This woman…will cause a break between me and her husband, who is a man with a future and under her control, and she will get him to join my enemies; or she herself will become intimate with them.' Or, 'This woman's husband is the seducer of the women of my harem; I will pay him back for that by seducing *his* wives, too.' Or, 'By the king's command, I will kill his enemy, who is hiding inside.' Or, 'My enemy is united with this woman's husband. Through her, I will get him to drink a potion. For these and similar reasons one may seduce even the wife of another man. But nothing rash should be done merely because of passion.[73]

Thus the *Kamasutra* accepts as a sufficient reason for adultery using a woman to protect a king or to kill an enemy—but passion is *not* an acceptable reason. As we have seen, the basic distrust of passion is a quality that the *Kamasutra* shares with the *Arthashastra*, and the other, rather far-fetched political motives are surely the direct legacy of Kautilya.

Both texts accept the concept of eight forms of legal marriage, as set forth by Manu: four more or less conventional rituals, followed by the demonic marriage (when the groom bribes the bride's relatives and carries her off), the centaur marriage (mutual consent and sexual union), the ogre's marriage (in which he carries the girl off, disregarding her screams, after he has maimed and murdered her male relatives), and the ghoul's marriage (when a man secretly has sex with a girl who is asleep, drunk, or out of her mind).[74] The *Arthashastra* ranks these eight marriages only slightly differently from Manu, raising the centaur marriage from sixth to fifth.[75]

But the *Kamasutra* does not bother to cite the first four, the conventional forms, at all, substituting for them the first half of an octet that it calls 'devious devices for weddings' and that contemporary readers might be more inclined to call 'rape'. The octet begins with four variations on the centaur marriage, in which the man tricks a virgin into running away with him and he himself performs a wedding ritual of some sort before deflowering her. The text then adds three more 'devices', beginning with two variants of the ghouls' marriage (dividing the category into one in which he deflowers her when she is drunk, and another when she is asleep) and, finally (omitting the demonic marriage entirely), the ogre's marriage.[76] In the *Kamasutra's* view, apparently, drugging a girl is not as bad as killing her relatives, and, predictably, it ranks as best of all the forms of marriage the centaur marriage of mutual desire, which the *Arthashastra* ranks fifth (and Manu ranks sixth). The *Kamasutra* even explicitly remarks that, 'Since mutual love is the fruit of wedding rites, therefore even the love-match wedding, though of middling rank, is respected as a means to a good end.'[77] (Even Manu grudgingly admits the appeal of the centaur marriage, stating that the best marriage for Brahmins is either of the first two forms of marriage, but that the best 'for the other classes is when they desire one another'.[78]) The *Kamasutra* at the very end, however, puts in a good word for dharma, in a verse citing the familiar rule for ranking the aims: 'With regard to maintaining dharma, each form of wedding is better than the one that follows it; but each time the preceding one is not possible, the following one should be used.'[79] Such verses in the *Kamasutra* restore a dharmic balance that the preceding prose has shattered.

Both the *Arthashastra* and the *Kamasutra* offer detailed, but not identical, lists of the skills of a courtesan.[80] Both texts speak about the use of male statues as dildos; the *Arthashastra*, specifying that the statues are of divine beings, disapproves of the practice,[81] while the *Kamasutra* thinks that such statues might come in useful in the harem.[82] The *Arthashastra* regards as sexually available a woman whom a man has saved when she has been carried away by a flood or left in the wilderness during a time of famine, or whom he has rescued from robbers or when she had been lost, abandoned, or left for dead.[83] Similarly, the *Kamasutra* suggests that a man might pick up a woman during the spectacle of a house on fire, the commotion after a robbery, or the invasion of the countryside by an army.[84]

Sometimes, rarely, the *Arthashastra* is more sexually permissive than the *Kamasutra*. The *Arthashastra* takes for granted the woman with many husbands,[85] who poses a problem even for the *Kamasutra*.[86] But almost always, the *Arthashastra* toes the *Dharmashastra* line on sexuality, often closely following Manu, where the *Kamasutra* diverges wildly from it.

The *Arthashastra* definition of the mastery of the senses speaks of the need for control, a concern that we have seen shared by the *Kamasutra*:

> Mastery over the senses consists of the senses—ear, skin, eye, tongue, and nose—not wandering inappropriately among sounds, touches, visible forms, tastes, and smells.[87]

Almost the exact same wording is turned on its head in the *Kamasutra* definition of kama:

> Kama, in general, consists in engaging the ear, skin, eye, tongue, and nose each in its own appropriate sensation, all

> under the control of the mind and heart driven by the conscious self.[88]

Where the *Arthashastra* does not want the senses to 'wander inappropriately' among the objects of the senses, which it enumerates, using this passage in the context of an argument that one should *give up* kama, the *Kamasutra* uses this same enumeration of the 'appropriate' uses of the senses in its argument *for the enjoyment of* kama— under the control of the conscious mind.

## SEX AND POLITICS

The Kautilyan base of the *Kamasutra*'s portrayal of the relationship between the sexes is expressed by the astounding statement, 'They say that sex is a form of quarrelling, because the very essence of desire is a contest, and its character is competitive.'[89] (The commentator, Yashodhara, explains the competition: 'Because the man and the woman each try to achieve their own desires by overcoming the other.') This agonistic view of sex is the essence of the *Kamasutra*. But who is the 'they' in 'they say'? Kautilya and his colleagues? And does Vatsyayana go along with this opinion? I think he does.

What happens to gender issues when the politics of the *Arthashastra* are applied to sex? The *Kamasutra*, under the influence of the *Arthashastra*, politicizes sex. Recall how Freud, in *The Interpretation of Dreams*, used the *political* idea of censorship as the basis of his idea of the censoring superego, which repressed sex more than anything else; for Freud, as for the *Kamasutra*, politics set the pattern for sex. It might have worked the other way, too; in other times and places, political texts, and in particular military texts (and much of the *Arthashastra* is about war), have drawn on sexual texts for their metaphors; Clive's invasion of India is often called 'the rape of India'. What is striking in the ancient Indian example is that this does not happen; politics gets into the *Kamasutra*, but sex does not get into the *Arthashastra*.

Much of the *Kamasutra* is devoted to trickery and deception of one sort or another: the man tricking the parents of a young girl, and tricking the girl; the married woman telling lies as she jockeys for power against her co-wives; the adulterer deceiving the woman's husband; the courtesan lying in order to get her customers to give her more money; various people using drugs to cloud the minds of their sexual objects. The resulting agonistic and duplicitous view of sex set the stage for much of the mythological substructure of later Indian erotic drama, poetry, and narrative.

The *Kamasutra* also establishes a code of acceptable sexual violence. The inflicting of physical pain by scratching, biting, and slapping is an important part of the sexual act, and so is its aftermath:

> When a woman sees the scars
> that nails have made on her hidden places,
> her love even for someone given up long ago
> becomes as tender as if it were brand new.
>
> ...
>
> And a man who is marked
> with the signs of nails in various places
> generally disturbs a woman's mind
> no matter how firm it may be.

> There are no keener means
> of increasing passion
> than acts inflicted
> with tooth and nail.[90]

The lover displays his or her scars as a warrior displays his battle scars. (The *Arthashastra*, by contrast, is concerned only about damage to women as property, primarily virgins but also, in passing, wives; it has no interest in protecting them from physical abuse of other kinds.)

More disturbing are the passages in the *Kamasutra* where women's exclamations are taken not as indications of their wish to escape pain being inflicted on them, but merely as part of a ploy designed to excite their male partners:

> Always, if a man tries to force his kisses and so forth on her, she moans and does the very same thing back to him. When a man in the throes of passion slaps a woman repeatedly, she uses words like 'Stop!' or 'Let me go!' or 'Enough!' or 'Mother!' and utters screams mixed with laboured breathing, panting, crying, and groaning. Those are the ways of groaning and slapping.[91]

These passages inculcate what we now recognize as the rape mentality—'her mouth says no, but her eyes say yes'—disregarding a woman's protests against physical abuse. Indeed, as we have seen, all three of our texts list rape as one of the worst, but still acceptable, forms of wedding devices. It should be noted here that the *Kamasutra* is in general remarkably favourable to women, but in this one instance, it reflects the darker side of the culture.

For two sharply contrasting attitudes to women can be traced in texts from the ancient period to the modern. The *dharmashastras*, insisting on the control and denigration of women, dominated conventional and legal attitudes to women particularly among the middle classes, while the *Kamasutra* tradition, with its far more liberal and complex admiration of women, never ceased to be appreciated by royal and upper-class merchant society. As it combined with other factors in the Hindu social system that led to a more general devaluing of women, the Kautilyan *Kamasutra* tradition contributed greatly to the culture of violence against women. The Indian version of the widespread idea that sex and women are dangerous does not of course originate in our two texts. It is well documented in ancient India in the *Mahabharata* and *Ramayana,* centuries before the period in question, and it dominates the misogynist traditions of Hindu dharma forever after. Both the *Kamasutra* and the *Arthashastra* may be responding to a society in which the political culture of spying and violence is already closely linked with sex, or the *Kamasutra* may have adopted these elements from the *Arthashastra*. But in any case, from then on sex and violence are joined at the hip. And the particular concept of a sexual relationship as a war with no Geneva conventions; a conflict in which the two parties try to deceive and outmanoeuvre one another; an encounter that requires ambassadors and truces; a battle in which the combatants conceal or display the wounds they receive (from bites, slaps, and scratches[92])—these major themes of Indian erotic fiction owe as much to the *Arthashastra* as to the *Kamasutra*.

The Kautilyan *Kamasutra* was a major influence upon the erotic literary traditions of India, particularly but not only court poetry, which revelled in the suffering of the abandoned heroine, the tragedies caused by careless or lustful messengers, the deceptions and betrayals.[93] The text played a less obvious but more important role in the eroticism of the bhakti tradition, the devotional tradition of Hinduism, with its emphasis on divine abandonment, deception, betrayal, and even physical violence. The surface metaphor of human desire, with its clichés of nail marks betraying infidelity, leads to the dark implications of divine desire, the god who is not merely caught with lipstick on his collar but who is not there for you as a god (the otiose god or *deus absconditus*, corresponding to the theme of *viraha*, painful longing for the absent lover), the god who desires your pain—walking on fire, swinging from hooks—and who deceives you with his power of illusion (*maya*). The apaché syndrome of Indian eroticism—'He is so cruel to me and I love him so'—inspired Nina Paley to use the torch song, 'Mean to Me',[94] for her modern version of the *Ramayana*.[95]

All of this may also be seen *in nuce* in the Kautilyan *Kamasutra*, which strongly influenced the way in which Indian culture developed its unique understanding of the politics of sex.

# 3

# THE MYTHOLOGY OF THE *KAMASUTRA*[1]

## MYTHOLOGICAL BACKGROUND

Vatsyayana tells some stories in the *Kamasutra* as part of a general mythological background. The very first chapter begins, after a few lines of introduction, with a classically mythological passage:

> When the Creator emitted his creatures, he first composed, in a hundred thousand chapters, the means of achieving the three aims of human life [dharma, artha, and kama[i]]: Manu the son of the Self-born One made one part of this into a separate work about dharma, Brihaspati made one about artha, and Nandin, the servant of the Great God Shiva, made a separate work of a thousand chapters, the *Kamasutra*, which Shvetaketu Auddalaki cut down to five hundred chapters. And then Babhravya of Panchala cut this down further to a hundred and fifty chapters.[2]

Manu the son of the Self-born One, the Creator, is the Indian Adam, a mythical creature but not a god; indeed, he defines the beginning of the human species, and is the mythical author of *The Laws of Manu.* The other two authors are gods: Brihaspati and Nandin. Brihaspati is the guru of the gods, the secretary or minister of defence, as it were, for Indra, the king of the gods, and, in his spare time, he is the planet Jupiter. Brihaspati is also the putative divine author of the *Arthashastra*, the textbook of political science—

---

i See chapter two, 'The Kautilyan *Kamasutra*'.

composed perhaps a century, or less, before the *Kamasutra*.[ii] To make the divine Brihaspati the author of the *Arthashastra* is to bring heaven down to earth (or, if you prefer, earth to heaven).

The third author, Nandin, is the ultimate source of Vatsyayana's *Kamasutra*, even as Brihaspati is the source of the *Arthashastra*. Yashodhara explains why he is appropriate for this role:

> Nandin is not some other person named Nandin, for the scripture says: 'While the Great God Shiva was experiencing the pleasures of union with his wife Uma for a thousand years as the gods count them, Nandin went to guard the door of their sleeping chamber and composed the *Kamasutra*.'[3]

Yashodhara is here making explicit the fact that the Nandin in question is actually a god, not merely a human named after a god (as people often are, in India and elsewhere). Nandin, a bull or a bull-headed deity, is the son of the Great God Shiva, and is often stationed to guard the door to his parents' room. In the earthly parallel to this situation, a statue of Nandin often guards the door to a temple of Shiva (and Uma).

The text then turns from gods to semi-mythical sages from ancient times, beginning with Shvetaketu, who is cited often in the *Kamasutra* as a sexual authority and who also has a mythology of his own, as the commentator, Yashodhara, reminds us:

> Once upon a time, there was so much seduction of other men's wives in the world that it was said: 'Women are all

---

ii See chapter two, 'The Kautilyan *Kamasutra*'.

> alike, just like cooked rice, your majesty. Therefore a man should not get angry with them nor fall in love with them, but just make love with them.'
>
> But [Shvetaketu] forbade this state of affairs, and so people said: '[Shvetaketu] forbade common people to take other people's wives.'
>
> Then, with his father's permission, Shvetaketu, who had amassed great ascetic power, happily composed this text, which distinguishes those who are eligible or ineligible for sex.[4]

This story is told at greater length in the *Mahabharata*,[5] and Shvetaketu is well-known as a hero of the Upanishads, the ancient Sanskrit philosophical texts that make the case for renunciation; in those texts, his father teaches him the central doctrines of Indian philosophy. It is surprising to find Shvetaketu here in the *Kamasutra*, cited as an expert sexologist, and this seeming incongruity may have inspired Vatsyayana to allude to, and Yashodhara to tell, this story here: it explains how a sage became simultaneously chaste, an enemy of male adultery, and an authority on sex.

Finally, the text mentions another mere human being: 'Dattaka made a separate book out of the sixth part of this work, about courtesans, which the courtesans de luxe of Pataliputra commissioned.'[6] But the commentary recites (or invents? I have not been able to find them in other sources) two stories about Dattaka, the second of which makes him supernatural, if not divine:

> One day Dattaka had the idea of learning the finest ways of the world, best known by courtesans. And so he went to the courtesans every day, and learned so well that they

> asked *him* to instruct *them*. A woman speaking on behalf of the courtesans said to him, 'Teach us how to give pleasure to men.' And because of that commission he made a separate book.

So the story goes. But another quite plausible story is also widely believed:

> Dattaka once touched Shiva with his foot in the course of a festival to bless a pregnant woman, and Shiva cursed him to become a woman; after a while he persuaded Shiva to rescind the curse and became a man again, and because of that double knowledge he made the separate book. If he had simply made a separate work out of what Babhravya had said, how would his own book have demonstrated such originality that people would say that he knew both flavours? But if the author of the *Kamasutra* had known that he had such double knowledge, then he would have said, 'Dattaka, who knew both flavours, made a separate book.' [7]

To touch anyone, let alone a god, with your foot, is an act of great disrespect and a common source of curses in India. And men are often, for a number of reasons, turned into women, and back again, in Hindu and Buddhist mythology; Narada, Bhangashvana and Ila are the most famous of the serial androgynes.[8] The 'double knowledge' of Dattaka refers to the comparative knowledge of sexuality, seen from both sides of the bed. It is an inspired move on the part of Yashodhara to make the author of this text a bisexual, who 'tastes both flavours' (I use 'bisexual' here both in its now popular sense of a person of fixed gender who has both male and female sexual partners, and in its older, mythological sense—of an androgyne or hermaphrodite).[iii] Yet this is also a move that greatly mitigates the strong female agency in the text: where Vatsyayana tells us that women had this text made, Yashodhara tells us that an extraordinary man knew more about the courtesans' art than they knew themselves.

All in all, there is a supernatural pedigree for the authors of this earthiest of all books. And there is also a supernatural pedigree for the very process of its recension, the boiling down of an enormous divine text into a manageable human text:

> Shvetaketu cut [the text] down to five hundred chapters. And then Babhravya of Panchala cut this down further to a hundred and fifty chapters...Charayana made a separate book about general observations, Suvarnanabha about sex, Ghotakamukha about virgins, Gonardiya about wives, Gonikaputra about other men's wives and Kuchumara about erotic esoterica. When many scholars had divided it into fragments in this way, the text was almost destroyed. Because the amputated limbs of the text that they divided are just parts of the whole, and because Babhravya's text is so long that it is hard to study, Vatsyayana condensed the entire subject matter into a small volume to make this *Kamasutra*.[9]

The word for 'scholars' (*acharyas*), normally a term of great respect, almost always has a pejorative tone in the *Kamasutra*, perhaps best translated as 'pedants'. The texts cited here no longer exist, but almost certainly existed at the time of Vatsyayana, since he often quotes directly from them (as does Yashodhara, much later). Other Hindu texts are also said to have been reduced from a supernatural source in this way,[10] perhaps on analogy with the human body, for,

iii See chapter five, 'The Third Nature'.

according to classical Hindu physiology, it takes ten drops of food to make a drop of digestive fluid, ten drops of that fluid to make a drop of blood, and ten drops of blood to make a drop of semen. The *Kamasutra* was reduced in this same way. A close parallel to this reasoning occurs in a Buddhist text about the woman who prepared milk-rice for the Buddha when he ended his long meditation after achieving enlightenment. She milked a thousand cows, and fed the milk to five hundred cows; then she milked those five hundred cows and fed the milk to two hundred and fifty, and so on, until she fed the milk of sixteen cows to eight. She used the milk of those eight cows to prepare the milk-rice for the Buddha.[11]

Vatsyayana himself seldom refers to the great gods, though he seems to assume their presence. We have seen him refer to Shiva and to Indra, the king of the gods and a god who, like Shiva, has a significantly phallic mythology. Indra's wife, Indrani, appears only in the name of a particular sexual position,[12] which can be translated as 'Junoesque' but is literally 'of Indrani'.[iv] Indrani resembles Juno, the wife of Jupiter, king of the Roman gods (or Hera, wife of the Greek Zeus), in many ways, including her own enormous sexual appetite and her jealousy about her husband's notorious adulteries.

Vatsyayana first refers to Indra in this not particularly erotic verse:

> Fate made Bali into
> an Indra, king of the gods,
> and fate hurled Bali back down,
> and fate is what will make him an Indra again.[13]

---

iv See chapter six, 'The Mare's Trap'.

And the commentary tells the story: Even though Bali was unworthy, because he was a demon, and should have been spurned, he ascended to the throne of Indra, king of the gods, and established himself there until the wheel of fortune turned around, and he was thrown out of that seat and hurled back down into Hell. But when the wheel of fortune turns back around again, it will once again send him out of Hell and back onto the throne of Indra. And so people say:

> Time ripens and cooks all beings,
> time absorbs all creatures,
> time is awake when all are asleep,
> for no one can fight against time.[14]

The commentary on the first book of the *Kamasutra* also mentions Indra, in passing, in the context of a myth about the divine embodiments of the three goals of life.[v]

These divine figures are scattered through the mythology of the first of the seven books of the *Kamasutra*, but they generally do not appear after that. Other gods, however, are occasionally mentioned in the later books. Vatsyayana never explicitly refers to Krishna, but one verse seems to suggest a famous myth of Krishna:

> They play the 'plough-handle' game, sing,
> and dance in the Lata way;
> they look at the circle of the moon
> with eyes moist and flickering with passion.[15]

And Yashodhara makes explicit the connection:

> It is said of the 'plough-handle' (Hallishaka):
> The 'plough-handle' is a dance

v See chapter two, 'The Kautiylan *Kamasutra*'.

with the women in a circle
and one man the leader,
like Krishna with the cowherd women.[16]

The incarnate god Krishna danced in a circle with the cowherd women, and by his magic powers created doubles of himself so that each woman thought she was dancing with him and making love with him.

## TALES TOLD TO ENCOURAGE WOMEN

The *Kamasutra* refers to a number of stories that it regards as so well known that it does not even bother to tell them. In many cases, Vatsyayana uses a myth to make a point quite different from its meaning in the texts from which he takes it. Often, he makes different points from the same myth when he cites it in different contexts; this is, of course, standard operating procedure in the world of mythmakers.[17] And the commentator Yashodhara tells us the versions that he knows of some, though not all, of these stories. Between the text and the commentary, we can excavate a rich sexual mythology.

The *Kamasutra* tells us how people told the myths, how they regarded them as relevant and didactically powerful. The basic plot of the *Kamasutra* is boy meets girl; boy sets out to get girl into bed, often with the help of a go-between; boy gets girl. In instructing the go-between messenger about ways to persuade a young girl to sleep with a man before he marries her, Vatsyayana says, 'And she tells the girl stories about other virgins of equal caste, such as Shakuntala, who found a husband by their own resolve and made love with great joy.'[18] The commentator here describes Shakuntala simply as 'the king's wife', and he says nothing at all about her when Vatsyayana mentions her a second time, as one of the women whose stories are to be told by the messenger trying to persuade a married woman (rather than, as in the first case, a virgin) to take a lover. On that occasion, Vatsyayana says: 'As the woman listens, the messenger tells her well-known, relevant stories, about Ahalya, Avimaraka, Shakuntala and others.'[19] These positive lists of women who did well by breaking the sexual rules[vi] seem to stand in sharp contrast with the negative lists of men who were destroyed by succumbing to passion.[vii] But, in fact, Shakuntala's story did not work out so well as Vatsyayana implies; Shakuntala suffers greatly in the version of her story told in the *Mahabharata*—the king impregnates her and then publicly denies and insults her; only years later does he acknowledge her.[20] (She suffers less, but still significantly, in the version told by the poet Kalidasa a few centuries later.[21])

The commentator does tell us about the other two people in this particular list, Ahalya and Avimaraka, of whom Ahalya is by far the more famous; she is to Indian mythology what Helen of Troy was to Greek mythology, and the *Ramayana* tells her story not once but twice, at the beginning and the end of the text. All that the commentator says here, where he is using her as the model of the successful adulteress, is: 'Ahalya was the wife of [the sage] Gautama; the king of the gods [Indra] fell in love with her and she desired him.'[22] But Vatsyayana has already mentioned Ahalya in the first

---

vi See chapter four, 'Women in the *Kamasutra*'.

vii See chapter two, 'The Kautilyan *Kamasutra*'.

chapter, in a very different context indeed, when he remarks that 'Indra, the king of the gods, with Ahalya...and many others afterwards were seen to fall into the thrall of desire and were destroyed.'[23] And there the commentator tells a longer story, not a story of encouragement at all, but a cautionary story:

> The king of the gods, Indra, was aroused by Ahalya; for when he saw her in the hermitage of her husband Gautama, he desired her. When Gautama returned with the fuel and sacred grass, his wife Ahalya hid Indra in the womb of the house, but just at that moment Gautama took his wife into the inside of the house, with an invitation to make love. Then he realized, with the magic gaze that he had achieved through yoga, that Indra had come there, and seeing that a third seat had been drawn up for him he said, 'What is this for, since only the two of us, my wife and I, are here?' Then he became suspicious, and by meditation he saw what had happened; in fury he cursed Indra: 'You yourself will have a thousand vaginas!' And so, even though Indra was the king of the gods, desire brought him to this sorry state, which was regarded as his destruction. Even to this day that mark that makes people call him 'Ahalya's Lover' has not vanished.[24]

Unique to this version is the suggestion that Ahalya's husband, Gautama, had intended to make love to her himself. Other versions of the story generally make it quite clear that Gautama is far too ascetic to do justice to his young wife in bed, and that is what makes her vulnerable to the king of the gods; Ahalya knows quite well that, even when Indra is disguised as Gautama, he is not Gautama, precisely because he wants to make love with her. Other variants, moreover, attribute the form of Indra's curse (to have the mark of vaginas all over his body) to the fact that Indra was caught in the 'womb' of Ahalya, not of the house; Gautama catches them *in flagrante*, the telltale piece of furniture being not a 'third seat drawn up' but the bed. Here, however, it appears that Gautama returns *before* Ahalya goes to bed with Indra, and so, of course, she is not punished, as she usually is, by being cursed to turn into a stone.

Unlike most other variants of this myth, moreover, Yashodhara's version does not mention that the king of the gods, Indra, took the form of Gautama to seduce Ahalya, making her, to some extent, less culpable: she did not intend to commit adultery, but was tricked into it, a factor that makes her story less useful for the purposes of the *Kamasutra*'s messenger. Yashodhara's version has been bowdlerized, cleaned up. Vatsyayana usually takes Indra as a sign for the excesses and dangers of uncontrolled desire; we have seen him mention Indra in the midst of a list of males—human, divine and demonic—who suffered from uncontrolled passion.[viii] Vatsyayana regards the story of Indra and Ahalya here, when he tells it as a caution to men, in a much more negative mode than when the messenger is later told to use it to persuade the woman,[25] and Yashodhara's longer gloss in the cautionary passage also adds much more detail, as a warning to a man about the trouble that desire can cause him. Clearly, Vatsyayana uses the tale of Ahalya (and Yashodhara tells it) in one way to warn men not to commit adultery, and in another way to encourage women to do it.

---

viii See chapter two, 'The Kautilyan *Kamasutra*'.

The third person in the list of people to be cited by the messenger encouraging married women to commit adultery is a man named Avimaraka; Yashodhara tells his story:

> The fire-priest instructed his wife to care for the fire. Agni, the god of fire, so desired her that he took on a form and arose out of the fire altar. When she became pregnant, her father-in-law, fearing a stain on the family, abandoned her in the forest. She gave birth to a son, whom the general of the Shabaras [a wild, savage tribe of mountaineers] raised as his own child. That son, in his childhood, played among the herds of sheep and goats and wandered around with them. By drinking their milk he became very strong, so strong that even though he was just a little child, he killed goats and sheep with his bare hands. And for that reason, the general gave him the appropriate name of Avimaraka ['Sheep-killer']. When Avimaraka reached the prime of his youth, one day an elephant attacked the daughter of a king who was sojourning in the forest, and Avimaraka killed the elephant and saved her. After that she fell in love with him and of her own will gave him her hand in marriage. These stories are relevant to a discussion of the seduction of other men's wives.[26]

Avimaraka is the hero of a Sanskrit play by Bhasa that follows this general plot-line. Bhasa glosses 'Avimaraka' as 'killer [*maraka*] of a demon who took the form of a sheep [*avi*]' and leaves out the whole episode of the genuine sheep. The *Kathasaritsagara*, too,[27] leaves out the sheep from its telling of the Avimaraka story. But one of the Buddhist Jatakas, the *Kunala Jataka*, #536, gives yet another connection with the sheep: the abandoned child drank sheep's milk in some way that killed the sheep. Since, however, Avimaraka is neither a woman nor an adulterer, it is not immediately clear how his tale is, as Yashodhara claims, relevant to a discussion of the seduction of other men's wives. Avimaraka does, according to Yashodhara, benefit from two seduced women, one married and seduced by someone else (this woman is his mother) and one unmarried and seduced by him. Is he dragged in through his association with these women who transgress sexual boundaries, because Vatsyayana could not think of any more women who benefited from adultery? Indeed, of *any* such women at all, since it is not at all clear how Shakuntala or Ahalya benefited from it, either?

I think, rather, the point is that Avimaraka was so handsome that the power of kama overcame all the objections that a princess might have had to marrying a man who appeared to be very low-caste (a tribal Shabara), a man who killed animals with his bare hands. In fact, the story may be based on a folk tale in which Avimaraka really was a tribal, a point that Bhasa, and the commentator on the *Kamasutra*, would then have erased in order to make the play more acceptable to a court audience.[28] In place of that story, these authors may simply have substituted a variant of the widespread myth of a boy of noble blood who is raised by animals, or the herders of animals, until he grows up and returns to claim his royal heritage. This is the story of Karna and of Krishna in India, as well as Kipling's Mowgli, and of Oedipus, Moses, Tarzan and many others.

Thus, even while the author of the *Kamasutra* pretends to give advice to persuade women to transgress, the actual content of the stories is designed to warn them, as they are explicitly said to warn men, to look before they leap.

Vatsyayana manifests his ambivalence about sexual freedom at many points in his book, particularly in the verses at the end of each chapter, which often raise doubts about matters that he has recommended in the prose passages. So, too, the stories that he refers to may be intended to raise doubts in the minds of the women being tempted to commit adultery, even while they are expressly said to be intended to quell such doubts.[29]

## TALES TOLD TO WARN MEN

Another supernatural item in this list of males undone by lust is 'Ravana with Sita'. This is the most famous of all tales of destructive lust, from the *Ramayana* [c. 200 BCE to 200 CE], which is perhaps why Yashodhara does not bother to tell the story of the abduction of Sita, wife of Rama, by the demon Ravana, and the subsequent destruction of Ravana. Yet Yashodhara mentions Ravana again when he expands on the reasons for passion, including 'fear of death, like the fear that afflicted (the celestial nymph) Rambha because of Ravana, who said to her, "If you do not satisfy my desire, I will kill you."'[30] The *Ramayana* tells how Ravana raped Rambha by threatening to kill her, but she cursed him so that he could never rape another woman again—a story that is told to explain why he could never violate Sita.

In this same list, Vatsyayana also mentions 'Kichaka with Draupadi', referring to a story about Draupadi, the heroine of the *Mahabharata* who had five husbands, the five sons of Pandu, under circumstances extenuated in various ways by various texts (both in the original Sanskrit version and in various retellings in Sanskrit and in vernacular languages) but never sufficiently to protect her from frequent slurs against her chastity. Yashodhara tells only part of the story: 'As for Kichaka, he is said to have been super powerful because he had the strength of a thousand elephants; but even he was destroyed by desire, for Bhima killed him when he lusted after Draupadi.'[31] 'Killed him' is putting it mildly: Bhima, dressed as a woman, beat Kichaka to such a pulp that when people found his mangled corpse the next morning they said, 'Where is his head?', 'Which are his hands?'[32]

The commentator mentions Draupadi again, a bit later, when Vatsyayana quotes another scholar (or pedant) who said that any married woman who is known to have had five men can be seduced without moral qualms,[33] for 'five men or more' (*pancha-jana*) is an expression for a crowd, a group of people (as in the *panchayat*, the quorum of a village). And Yashodhara adds: 'If, besides her own husband, [a woman] has five men as husbands, she is a loose woman and eligible for everyone who has a good reason. Draupadi, however, who had Yudhishthira and the others as her own husbands, was not eligible for other men. How could one woman have several husbands? Ask the authors of the *Mahabharata*!' So, once again, the same character appears in two different passages that make two different points for two different genders: Draupadi with Kichaka is a warning for lustful males, but Draupadi with her five husbands is a challenge for chaste females.

To return to the list of males undone by passion, we are left with one more mortal, a king named Dandakya,[ix] and Yashodhara tells his story:

---

ix See chapter two, 'The Kautilyan *Kamasutra*'.

> Dandakya was out hunting when he saw the daughter of the Brahmin Bhargava in his hermitage. Overwhelmed by passion, he took her up in his chariot and carried her off. When Bhargava returned with the fuel and sacred grass that he had gone off to fetch, and did not see her, he meditated to learn what had happened and then he cursed the king. As a result, Dandakya and his entire family and kingdom were covered by a dust-storm and died. Even today they sing about that place, the Dandaka Wilderness.[34]

Yashodhara also refers to Dandakya just a few lines later, as an example of a man for whom 'pleasure destroys the other two [goals] when it involves women of a higher class, or other excesses'.[35]

All of these seductions involved tricks, which the *Kamasutra* does not mention: Indra pretended to be Ahalya's husband; Kichaka was foiled (and killed) when a man took the place of the woman he intended to seduce; and Ravana masqueraded as an ascetic to abduct Sita, while (in many tellings after the first Sanskrit version) a shadow Sita took the place of the Sita that Ravana thought he had abducted.[36] All illusory seductions, they were all the more deadly for that.

The rest of the mythology of the *Kamasutra*, which punctuates the entire text, consists primarily of warnings against the abuse of the power of sex, warnings that we have already seen applied to mythological figures and that now reappear in the human realm. For example, in warning against the use of certain violent forms of slapping (called the 'wedge', the 'scissor' and the 'drill'), Vatsyayana says:

> The King of the Cholas killed Chitrasena, a courtesan, by using the 'wedge' during sex. And the Kuntala king

> Shatakarni Shatavahana killed his queen, Malayavati, by using the 'scissor'. Naradeva, whose hand was deformed, blinded a dancing-girl in one eye by using the 'drill' clumsily.[37]

And Yashodhara explains:

> He embraced Chitrasena so tightly, at the start of their love-making, that she suffered greatly, because she was so delicate. And even when he realized her condition, and knew that she had to be handled delicately, he was so blind with passion that he did not take account of his own strength and destroyed her by using a 'wedge' on her chest.
>
> Shatakarna's son Shatavahana, born in the territory of Kuntala, saw his queen, Malayavati, one day when she had not long recovered from an illness and did not have her full strength, but was dressing for the festival of Kama. Passion arose in him and he made love to her, but his mind was carried away by passion and by using an excessively powerful 'scissor' on her chest, he killed her.
>
> Naradeva was the general of the Pandya king. His hand had been deformed by a blow from a sword. When he saw Chitralekha, a dancing girl, dancing at the king's residence, his passion was aroused, and when he made love with her, blind with passion, he used the 'drill' clumsily because of his lame hand; he missed her cheek and instead hit her eye, blinding her in that eye.[38]

The kings who commit these excesses are all from South India, where Vatsyayana (a North Indian) generally locates sexual excess. In contrast with such figures as Ravana and Ahalya, these kings are not well-known to Sanskrit mythology.

Another excessive king is an adulterer:

> 'For when Abhira, the Kotta king, went to another man's home, a washerman employed by the king's brother killed him. And the superintendant of horses killed Jayasena the king of Varanasi.' So it is said.[39]

The 'it is said' may cast some doubt on this pair of adulterers, but not necessarily so. Yashodhara tells just a bit more (which I have indicated in added italics):

> *In Gujarat* there is a place named Kotta, whose king, named Abhira, went to another man's house *in order to sleep with the wife of Vasumitra, the head warrior.* There, a guard employed by his brother, *who deserved the kingdom,* killed him. Jayasena the king of Varanasi [too] *had gone into another man's house to make love with that man's wife.*[40]

The commentator has added the details of individual people and places, and the sexual purpose of the housebreaking. Evidently these kings do not have the licence that many European kings, for instance, were able to make use of licentiously. Elsewhere, Vatsyayana insists, in a verse:

> Kings and ministers of state do not enter into other men's homes,
> For the whole populace sees what they do and imitates it.
> The three worlds watch the sun rise
> and so they too rise;
> then they watch the sun moving
> and they too start to act.[41]

But then Vatsyayana descends from verse to prose, and from the ideal to the actual: 'Therefore, because it is impossible and because they would be blamed, such men do nothing frivolous. But when they cannot help doing it, they employ stratagems.'[42]

So much for the mythology of warning kings.

But the *Kamasutra* persists in expressing both cautionary tales for men and exhortations to women through the citation of well-known and, occasionally, lesser-known myths.

# 4

# WOMEN IN THE *KAMASUTRA*[1]

The assumption that the intended reader of the *Kamasutra* is male persists in popular culture today, where Vinod Verma, apparently hoping to rectify this imbalance, published *The Kamasutra for Women: The Modern Woman's Way to Sensual Fulfilment and Health*, applying Ayurvedic techniques to female heterosexual relationships; and in 2002 there was *The Woman's Kamasutra*, by Nitya Lacroix; and then the *Kama Sutra para la Mujer*. But there is no need for such books.[2] The *Kamasutra* is for women—it was intended to be used by women, and has much to offer to women even today.

Vatsyayana argues at some length that some women, at least, should read this text, and that others should learn its contents in other ways:

> A woman should study the *Kamasutra* and its subsidiary arts before she reaches the prime of her youth, and she should continue when she has been given away, if her husband wishes it. Scholars say: 'Since females cannot grasp texts, it is useless to teach women this text.' Vatsyayana says: But women understand the practice, and the practice is based on the text. This applies beyond this specific subject of the *Kamasutra*, for throughout the world, in all subjects, there are only a few people who know the text, but the practice is within the range of everyone. And a text, however far removed, is the ultimate source of the practice.

> 'Grammar is a science,' people say. Yet the sacrificial priests, who are no grammarians, know how to gloss the words in the sacrificial prayers. 'Astronomy is a science,' they say. But ordinary people perform the rituals on the days when the skies are auspicious. And people know how to ride horses and elephants without studying the texts about horses and elephants. In the same way, even citizens far away from the king do not step across the moral line that he sets. The case of women learning the *Kamasutra* is like those examples. And there are also women whose understanding has been sharpened by the text: courtesans and the daughters of kings and state ministers.[3]

This is an important text, for it argues for the method by which the *Kamasutra* (and indeed, other Sanskrit texts) would have been known not only by women, but by the wider population in general; such knowledge was by no means limited to men, or women, who knew Sanskrit.

The eighty century CE playwright Bhavabhuti, in his *Malatimadhava*, depicts women actually citing the *Kamasutra* (2.2.6-7). At the start of act seven, when a woman complains that her friend was raped by her husband on the wedding night, she changes from the dialect in which she is speaking (as most women in Sanskrit plays do) and 'resorts to Sanskrit' (as the stage directions indicate) to say, 'The authors of the *Kamasutra* warn, "Women are like flowers, and need to be enticed very tenderly. If they are taken by force by men who have not yet won their trust they become women who hate sex."' This is important evidence not only of the common knowledge of the *Kamasutra* in literary circles, but of the use of it by women who knew Sanskrit as well as the dialects in which they conventionally spoke. It is also evidence that the

*Kamasutra* was regarded as a counterforce to the prevalent culture of sexual violence.[i]

In addition to this general expectation that all women should know all of the *Kamasutra*, particular parts of the book were evidently designed to be used by women. Book Three devotes one episode to advice to virgins trying to get husbands,[4] and Book Four consists of instructions for wives. Book Six is said to have been commissioned by the courtesans of Pataliputra, presumably for their own use.[5]

## WOMEN'S RIGHTS

The *Kamasutra* reveals relatively liberal attitudes to women's education and sexual freedom. To appreciate this, it is useful briefly to recall the attitudes to women in two important texts that precede it, the *Laws of Manu* and the *Arthashastra*.[ii] Kautilya, the author of the *Arthashastra*, is far more liberal than Manu. He takes for granted the woman with several husbands,[6] who is unimaginable for Manu and poses a problem even for the permissive *Kamasutra*.[7] Kautilya is also more lenient than Manu when it comes to divorce and widow remarriage; where Manu does not allow either of these options for a woman whose husband has died, Kautilya gives a woman some control over her property, which consists of jewellery without limit and a small maintenance;[8] she continues to own these after her husband's death—unless she remarries, in which case she forfeits them, with interest,

i See chapter two, 'The Kautilyan *Kamasutra*'. The *Malatimadhava* also shows the strong influence of Kautilya's *Arthashastra* in the description of court politics.

ii See chapter two, 'The Kautilyan *Kamasutra*'.

or settles it all on her sons.[9] In these ways and others, Kautilya allows women more independence than Manu does. But both of them greatly limit women's sexual and economic freedom.

The *Kamasutra*, predictably, is far more open-minded than Manu about women's access to household funds, and about divorce and widow remarriage. The absolute power that the wife in the *Kamasutra* has in running the household's finances[10] stands in sharp contrast with Manu's statement that a wife 'should not have too free a hand in spending'[11] and his cynical remark that, 'No man is able to guard women entirely by force, but they can be safely guarded if kept busy amassing and spending money, engaging in purification, attending to their duties, cooking food and looking after the furniture.'[12] And when it comes to female promiscuity, Vatsyayana is light years ahead of Manu. Vatsyayana cites an earlier authority on the best places to pick up married women, of which the first is 'on the occasion of visiting the gods' and others include a sacrifice, a wedding, or a religious festival.[13] Secular opportunities involve playing in a park, bathing or swimming, or theatrical spectacles. More extreme occasions are offered by the spectacle of a house on fire, the commotion after a robbery, or the invasion of the countryside by an army.[14] Somehow I don't think Manu would approve of the man in question meeting married women at all, let alone using devotion to the gods as an occasion for it, or equating such an occasion with spectator sports like hanging around watching houses burn down.

## WOMEN'S SEXUALITY

Vatsyayana presents an argument in favour of female orgasm far more subtle than views that prevailed in Europe until very recently indeed, and certainly worlds above the attitudes of his predecessors, whose cockamamie ideas he quotes. He tells the man how to recognize when a woman has reached a climax—or, perhaps, if we assume (as I think we should) that the text is intended for women, too, he is telling the woman how to fake it:

> The signs that a woman is reaching her climax are that her limbs become limp, her eyes close, she loses all sense of shame, and she takes him deeper and deeper inside her. She flails her hands about, sweats, bites, will not let him get up, kicks him, and continues to move over the man even after he has finished making love.[15]

Vatsyayana argues that women have orgasms just like men; Yashodhara supports Vatsyayana's position with a poem of unknown provenance:

> A woman's sensual pleasure is two-fold:
> the scratching of an itch and the pleasure of melting.
> The melting, too, is two-fold:
> the flowing and the ejaculation of the seed.
> She gets wet just from the flowing,
> and her sensual pleasure of ejaculation comes from being churned.
> But when a woman is carried away by her sexual energy,
> she ejaculates at the end, it is said, just like a man.[16]

From this, Vatsyayana concludes: 'Therefore the woman should be treated in such a way that she achieves her sexual climax first.'[17] And he quotes authorities that insist that a woman emits semen in order to conceive a child. This belief gives women an equal share in the making of a child, a viewpoint that contradicts the assumption, widespread in ancient India, that a woman contributes to the embryo not semen but simply menstrual blood, which, since it takes ten drops of blood to make one drop of semen, would mean that the woman contributes to the child only one-tenth as much as the man.

Vatsyayana also knew about the G-spot (named after the German gynaecologist Ernst Graefenberg): 'When her eyes roll when she feels him in certain spots, he presses her in just those spots.'[18] Vatsyayana quotes a predecessor who said, 'This is the secret of young women'—and, indeed, it remained a secret in Europe for quite a few centuries, in part because Sir Richard Burton mistranslated it: 'Here *Suvarnanabha* says that while a man is doing to the woman what he likes best during congress, he should always make a point of pressing those parts of her body on which she turns her eyes.'[19] Here, as elsewhere, Burton wrongly followed the commentary, which suggests the reading of 'she turns her eyes', in the sense of looking at something, instead of the eyes rolling. Burton also wrongly attributes the whole thing to Suvarnanabha (to whom Vatsyayana attributes only the afterthought generalization about 'the secret of young women', which Burton omits entirely). By following one part of the commentary, Burton has missed one point of the passage, how to locate the G-spot, and by inserting, gratuitously, the phrase 'what he likes best', he has totally missed the larger point, the importance of learning how to give a woman an orgasm.

## SEXUAL FREEDOM

The *Kamasutra* assumes a kind of sexual freedom for women that would have appalled Manu but simply does not interest Kautilya. Vatsyayana is a strong advocate for women's sexual pleasure. He tells us that a woman who does not experience the pleasures of love may hate her man and leave him for another.[20] If, as the context suggests, this woman is married, the casual manner in which Vatsyayana suggests that she leave her husband is in sharp contrast to the position assumed by the *Laws of Manu*: 'A virtuous wife should constantly serve her husband like a god, even if he behaves badly, freely indulges his lust and is devoid of any good qualities.'[21] The *Kamasutra* also acknowledges that women could use magic to control their husbands, though Vatsyayana regards this as a last resort.[22] He casually mentions, among the women that one might not only sleep with but marry,[23] not only 'second-hand' women (whom Manu despises as 'previously had by another man') but widows: 'a widow who is tormented by the weakness of the senses…finds, again, a man who enjoys life and is well-endowed with good qualities'.[24]

Vatsyayana dismisses with one or two short verses the possibility that the purpose of the sexual act is to produce children; one of the things that make sex for human beings different from sex for animals, he points out, is the fact that human women, unlike animals, have sex even when they are not in their fertile period.[25] Given the enormous emphasis that Manu and all the other dharma texts place on having sex *only* to produce children, the *Kamasutra*'s attitude here is extraordinary.[iii]

---

iii See 'Introduction: Redeeming the *Kamasutra*'.

Vatsyayana's discussion of the reasons why women become unfaithful rejects the traditional patriarchal party line that one finds in most Sanskrit texts, a line that punishes very cruelly indeed any woman who sleeps with a man other than her husband (cutting off her nose, for instance). Manu assumes that every woman desires every man she sees: 'Good looks do not matter to them, nor do they care about youth; "A man!" they say, and enjoy sex with him, whether he is good-looking or ugly'.[26] The *Kamasutra* takes off from this same assumption, but then limits it to *good-looking* men and modifies it with an egalitarian, if cynical, formulation: 'A woman desires any attractive man she sees, and, in the same way, a man desires a woman. But, after some consideration, the matter goes no further.'[27] The text does go on to state that women have less concern for morality than men have; it does assume that women don't think about anything but men; and it is written in the service of the hero, the would-be adulterer, who reasons, if all women are keen to give it away, why shouldn't one of them give it to him?

But the author empathetically imagines various women's reasons not to commit adultery (of which consideration for dharma comes last, as an afterthought), and the would-be seducer takes the woman's misgivings seriously, even if only to disarm her:

> Here are the causes of a woman's resistance: love for her husband, regard for her children, the fact that she is past her prime, or overwhelmed by unhappiness, or unable to get away; or she gets angry and thinks, 'He is propositioning me in an insulting way'; or she fears, 'He will soon go away. There is no future in it; his thoughts are attached to someone else'; or she is nervous, thinking, 'He does not

> conceal his signals'; or she fears, 'His advances are just a tease'; or she is diffident, thinking, 'How glamorous he is'; or she becomes shy when she thinks, 'He is a man-about-town, accomplished in all the arts'; or she feels, 'He has always treated me just as a friend'; or she cannot bear him, thinking, 'He does not know the right time and place,' or she does not respect him, thinking, 'He is an object of contempt'; or she despises him when she thinks, 'Even though I have given him signals, he does not understand'; or she feels sympathy for him and thinks, 'I would not want anything unpleasant to happen to him because of me'; or she becomes depressed when she sees her own shortcomings, or afraid when she thinks, 'If I am discovered, my own people will throw me out'; or scornful, thinking, 'He has grey hair'; or she worries, 'My husband has employed him to test me'; or she has regard for dharma.[28]

Just as he had imagined the reasons why a woman might be positively inclined to betray her husband,[iv] Vatsyayana here brilliantly imagines the resistance of a woman who is tempted to commit adultery, and his thinking is both more subtle and more thorough than the psychologizing of novelists like Gustave Flaubert and John Updike. This discussion is ostensibly intended to teach the male reader of the text how to manipulate and exploit such women: 'A man should eliminate, from the very beginning, whichever of these causes for rejection he detects in his own situation.'[29] But, perhaps inadvertently, it provides a most perceptive exposition of the reasons why women hesitate to begin an affair.

---

iv See chapter two, 'The Kautilyan *Kamasutra*'.

And the *Kamasutra* is equally informative about women's (more precisely, courtesans') thinking about ways of ending an affair. It describes the devious devices that the courtesan uses to make her lover leave her, rather than simply kicking him out:

> She does for him what he does not want, and she does repeatedly what he has criticized. She talks about things he does not know about. She shows no amazement, but only contempt, for the things he does know about. She intentionally distorts the meaning of what he says. She laughs when he has not made a joke, and when he has made a joke, she laughs about something else. When he is talking, she looks at her entourage with sidelong glances and slaps them. And when she has interrupted his story, she tells other stories. She talks in public about the bad habits and vices that he cannot give up. She asks for things that should not be asked for. She punctures his pride. She ignores him. She criticizes men who have the same faults. And she stalls when they are alone together. And at the end, the release happens of itself.[30]

A little inside joke that may not survive the cross-cultural translation is the word used for 'release'—*moksha*—which generally refers to a person's spiritual release from the world of transmigration; there may be an intended irony in its use here to designate the release of a man from a woman's thrall. The rest comes through loud and clear, however: the woman employs what some would call passive-aggressive behaviour to indicate that it is time to hit the road, Jack. There is no male equivalent for this passage, presumably because a man would not have to resort to such subterfuges: he would just throw the woman out. The woman's method is an example of what James Scott has taught us to recognize as the 'weapons of the weak', the 'arts of resistance'.[31]

## WOMEN'S VOICES

Passages such as the woman's thoughts about beginning an affair, or a courtesan's thoughts about ending one, may express a woman's voice, or at least a woman's point of view. The *Kamasutra* often quotes women in direct speech, expressing views that men are advised to take seriously, and it is clearly sympathetic to women, particularly to what they suffer from inadequate husbands.[32] But if parts of the text are directed toward women, is it also the case that they reflect women's voices? Certainly not always. For, while the *Kamasutra* quotes women in direct speech, we also encounter the paradox of women's voices telling us, through the text, that women had no voices.

Male texts may merely engage in a ventriloquism that attributes to women viewpoints that in fact serve male goals.[33] The *Kamasutra* not only assumes an official male voice (the voice of Vatsyayana) but denies that women's words truly represent their feelings.[v] Vatsyayana also takes for granted the type of rape that we now associate with sexual harassment, as he describes men in power who can take whatever women they want:

> A young village headman, or a king's officer, or the son of the superintendent of farming, can win village women just with a word, and then libertines call these women adulteresses. And in the same manner, the man in charge of the cowherds may take the women of the cowherds; the

v See chapter two, 'The Kautilyan *Kamasutra*'.

> man in charge of threads [presumably the supervisor of women engaged in sewing and weaving] may take widows, women who have no man to protect them, and wandering women ascetics; the city police-chief may take the women who roam about begging, for he knows where they are vulnerable, because of his own night-roamings; and the man in charge of the market may take the women who buy and sell.[34]

These women, at least, have absolutely no voice at all, let alone agency.

We must admit that we find women's voices in the *Kamasutra* carrying meanings that have value for us only by transcending, if not totally disregarding, the original context. Were we to remain within the strict bounds of the historical situation, we could not notice the women's voices speaking against their moment in history, perhaps even against their author. Only by asking our own questions, which the author may not have considered at all, can we see that his text does contain many answers to them, fortuitously embedded in other questions and answers that were more meaningful to him.

# 5

# THE THIRD NATURE: GENDER INVERSIONS IN THE *KAMASUTRA*[1]

## TRADITIONAL AND INVERTED INDIAN CONCEPTS OF GENDER

If we read carefully, the *Kamasutra* reveals surprisingly modern ideas about gender, unexpectedly subtle stereotypes of feminine and masculine natures, and far more complex views of homosexual acts than are suggested by other texts of this period.

We can learn a lot about conventional and unconventional Hindu ideas of gender from the *Kamasutra*. First, the expected: Vatsyayana tells us that, 'By his physical nature, the man is the active agent and the young woman is the passive locus. The man is aroused by the thought, "I am taking her," the young woman by the thought, "I am being taken by him."'[2] These gender stereotypes—the passive woman, active man—underlie other gender arguments in the text, too. Vatsyayana tells us what he thinks of as typically female behaviour: 'dress, chatter, grace, emotions, delicacy, timidity, innocence, frailty and bashfulness'. The closest he has to a word for our 'gender' is *tejas*, a Sanskrit term designating light and heat, rather as we might say, 'It is what someone shines at,' or, perhaps, 'natural talent' or 'glory':

> A man's natural talent is
> his roughness and ferocity;
> a woman's is her lack of power
> and her suffering, self-denial and weakness.[3]

The commentator, Yashodhara, expands this verse by explaining that people can, however, deviate from these norms:

> Sometimes, but not always, there is an exchange when they make love, out of the pull of passion or according to the practice of the place. Then the woman abandons her own ways and changes to what the man has a natural talent for, doing the slapping, while the man abandons his own way, of slapping the woman, and takes up her ways, moaning and screaming. But after a short time, they change back. And in the absence of passion or this particular technique, they do it just as before, and there is no occasion to switch.

What Europeans call the 'missionary position' is the assumed norm in most Hindu texts; indeed, it begins in the *Rig Veda*, which, in describing the original creation of the universe, imagines the missionary position: male seed-placers, giving-forth, above, and female powers below, receiving beneath.[4] The *Kamasutra* mentions this position briefly, but without enthusiasm, listing it among all the other, more exotic positions that 'take practice': 'In the "cup", both partners stretch out both of their two legs straight. There are two variants: the "cup lying on the side" or "the cup supine".'[5] And the commentator scornfully remarks, 'How does he penetrate her in this position? It is so easy that there is nothing to worry about!.' So much for the position that Europeans generally regarded as the default position, as it were.

But the *Kamasutra* tells us that people do switch genders sometimes—when they engage in the sexual position with the woman on top, which is heavily laden with gender implications for women. Most Sanskrit texts refer to the position with the woman on top as the 'perverse' or 'reversed' or 'topsy turvy' position (*viparitam*), the wrong way around. Vatsyayana, however, never uses this pejorative term. Instead, he refers to the woman-on-top position only with the verb 'to play the man's role' (*purushayitva*). He acknowledges that people do, sometimes, reverse gender roles,[6] and this switch of 'natural talents' is precisely what happens when the woman is on top: 'She does to him in return now whatever acts he demonstrated before. And, at the same time, she indicates that she is embarrassed and exhausted and wishes to stop.'[7] Yashodhara spells out the gender complications:

> All of this activity is said to be done with a woman's natural talent. The acts he demonstrated before are acts that he executed with roughness and ferocity, the man's natural talent; she now does these acts against the current of her own natural talent. She hits him hard, with the back of her hand and so forth, demonstrating her ferocity. And so, in order to express the woman's natural talent, even though she is not embarrassed, nor exhausted, and does not wish to stop, she indicates that she is embarrassed and exhausted and wishes to stop.

Now, since Vatsyayana insists that the woman 'unveils her own feelings completely when her passion drives her to get on top',[8] the feelings of the woman when she plays the man's role seem to be both male and female. Or, rather, as the commentator explains, when she acts like a man, she pretends to be a man and then she pretends to be a woman. Thus Vatsyayana acknowledges a woman's active agency and challenges her stereotyped gender role.

The poet Amaru, in the seventh or eighth century CE, wrote a verse about a girl who forgets herself, and forgets her womanly modesty, as she makes love on top of her male partner, but then, as her memory returns, and with it her sense of shame, she suddenly becomes aware of her own body and releases [*mukta*] first her male nature and then her lover.[9] The thirteenth-century commentator Arjunavarmadeva glosses the verse, in part, like this:

> An impassioned woman in the woman-on-top position abandons, first, maleness, and, right after that, her lover. What happened? She perceived her own body, which she had not recognized at all while she was impassioned. Only later is there any mention of the distinction between being male or female. She is described as becoming modest only at the onset of memory.[10]

The sequence here seems to be that she takes on a male nature, loses her natural female modesty, suddenly regains her memory, regains her modesty, recognizes her female body, lets go of her male nature and lets go (physically) of the man. The inter-relationship between gendered actions (male on top, female underneath), gendered natures (males rough, females modest) and gendered bodies, together with the loss and recovery of a sense of one's own body balanced against the holding and releasing of the body of a sexual partner, is complex indeed. (It becomes even more complex when we recall that 'release' [*mukta*] is from the same root as *moksha*, the word that, on the one hand, as we have seen,[i] Vatsyayana uses for the courtesan's technique of getting rid

---

i See chapter four, 'Women in the *Kamasutra*'.

of an unwanted lover and, on the other hand, in a religious context, signifies ultimate liberation from the wheel of rebirth.)

## SAME-SEX MEN

What about more extreme challenges to gender roles? What, for instance, does the text have to say about people who engage in homosexual acts? Classical Hinduism is in general significantly silent on the subject of homoeroticism, but Hindu mythology does drop hints from which we can excavate a pretty virulent homophobia. The dharma textbooks, too, either ignore or stigmatize homosexual activity. Male homoerotic activity was punished, albeit mildly: a ritual bath[11] or the payment of a small fine[12] was often a sufficient atonement.

But the ascetic aspects of Hinduism create a violent dichotomy between marriage, in which sexuality is tolerated for the sake of children, and a renunciant priesthood, in which asceticism is idealized and sexuality entirely rejected, or at least recycled. In this taxonomy, homosexual love represents what Mary Douglas has taught us to recognize as a major category error, something that doesn't fit into any existing conceptual cubbyhole, 'matter out of place'—in a word, dirt.[13] Traditional Hindu mythology regards homosexual union not, like heterosexual marriage, as a compromise between two goals in tension (procreation and asceticism), but as a mutually polluting combination of the worst of both worlds (sterility and lust). The myths, therefore, seldom explicitly depict homosexual acts at all, let alone sympathetically.

The Sanskrit word *kliba* has traditionally been translated as 'eunuch' but almost certainly did not mean 'eunuch', since eunuchs—in the particular sense of men intentionally castrated in order to serve as guardians in the royal harem—did not exist in India before the Turkish presence in the ninth century and, therefore, cannot be recorded in texts such as the *Mahabharata*, composed long before that date. Men were castrated in punishment for various crimes in ancient India (and animals were gelded to control them), but such men were not employed as eunuchs. '*Kliba*', rather, includes a wide range of meanings under the general rubric of 'a man who does not act the way a man should act', a man who fails to be a man, a defective male. It is a catch-all term that traditional Hindus coined to indicate a man who is in their terms sexually dysfunctional (or in ours, sexually challenged), including someone who was sterile, impotent, castrated, a transvestite, a man who had oral sex with other men, who had anal sex, a man with mutilated or defective sexual organs, a hermaphrodite, or, finally, a man who produced only female children. Often it has the vaguely pejorative force of 'wimp'. Thus, when Krishna, the incarnate god in the *Bhagavad Gita*, wishes to stir the martial instincts of the conscience-stricken human hero Arjuna, he says to him, 'Stop behaving like a *kliba*!'[14]

The *Kamasutra* departs from the dharmic view of homosexuality in significant ways. It does not use the pejorative term *kliba* at all, but speaks instead of a 'third nature' (*tritiya prakriti*) or perhaps a 'third sexuality' in the sense of sexual behaviour:

> There are two sorts of third nature, in the form of a woman and in the form of a man. The one in the form of

> a woman imitates a woman's dress, chatter, grace, emotions, delicacy, timidity, innocence, frailty and bashfulness. The act that is [generally] done in the sexual organ is done in her mouth, and they call that 'oral sex'. She gets her sexual pleasure and erotic arousal as well as her livelihood from this, living as a courtesan. That is the person of the third nature in the form of a woman.[15]

The *Kamasutra* says nothing more about this cross-dressing male, with his stereotypical female gender behaviour, but it discusses the fellatio technique of the closeted man of the third nature in considerable sensual detail, in the longest consecutive passage in the text describing a physical act, and with what might even be called gusto:

> The one in the form of a man, however, conceals her desire when she wants a man and makes her living as a masseur. As she massages the man, she caresses his two thighs with her limbs, as if she were embracing him. Then she becomes more boldly intimate and familiar...pretending to tease him about how easily he becomes excited and laughing at him. If the man does not urge her on, even when she has given this clear sign and even when it is obvious that he is aroused, she makes advances to him on her own. If the man urges her to go on, she argues with him and only unwillingly continues.[16]

And so forth, and so on. This is a remarkably explicit analysis of the mentality of the closet, the extended double entendre of an act that is cleverly designed to appear sexually innocent to a man who does not want, or does not want to admit that he wants, a homosexual encounter, but is an explicit invitation to a man who is willing to admit his desire for such an encounter. And a massage is a massage in the *Kamasutra*: 'Some people think that massaging is also a kind of close embrace, because it involves touching. But Vatsyayana says: 'No. For a massage takes place at a particular time set aside, has a different use, and is not enjoyed by both partners in the same way.'[17] Or is it? Consider this: 'But when a woman who is giving the man a massage makes sure he has understood her signals and rests her face on his thighs as if she had no desire but was overcome by sleep, and then kisses his thighs, that is called a kiss [of] "making advances."'[18]

The legitimacy of this person of the 'third nature' is supported by a casual remark in the passage describing the four sorts of love, and the contexts in which they arise. One of the four types is called 'The love that comes from erotic arousal', and it is said to arise from the imagination, not in response to any object of the senses: 'It can be recognized in the course of oral sex with a woman or with a person of the third nature, or in various activities such as kissing.'[19] The commentary expands upon this but, significantly, leaves out the reference to the person of the third nature and refers only to a female partner: 'Erotic arousal also comes from kissing, embracing, scratching, biting, slapping and so forth; at the moment of sexual pleasure, the person performing these acts experiences a mental love, and the *woman* for whom they are done also experiences a mental, rather than merely physical, love, because of the imaginative power of passion directed to each spot that is being stimulated.' Here, as so often, the later commentary has closed down one of the options.

One remark, in a passage warning the bridegroom not to be too shy with his shy bride, suggests that some people disapprove of men of the third nature: '[Certain scholars] say, "If the girl sees that the man has not spoken a word for three nights, like a pillar, she will be discouraged and will despise him, as if he were someone of the third nature."'[20] So, judgmentalism appears to creep in after all. But when we look closer we see that the people who make this judgment are the 'scholars' with whom Vatsyayana almost always disagrees,[ii] as he does here, for he goes on to remark: 'Vatsyayana says: He begins to entice her and win her trust, but he still remains sexually continent. When he entices her he does not force her in any way, for women are like flowers, and need to be enticed very tenderly. If they are taken by force by men who have not yet won their trust they become women who hate sex. Therefore he wins her over with gentle persuasion.'[21] This is the sort of man whom the wrong sort of scholar, but not Vatsyayana, might fear that some people might stigmatize as someone of the third nature. It is evidence, all the more impressive for being so casual, of the prevalent homophobia of that time and place.

Men of the third nature are always designated by the pronoun 'she', basically because the word 'nature' is feminine in Sanskrit (as it, and most abstract nouns, are also in Latin and Greek). Indeed, the idea of a third gender, rather than a binary division, may come from the basic habit of Indo-European languages to assign three genders—neuter as well as masculine and feminine—to all nouns. Yet the very use of the word 'third'—which clearly implies a previous 'first' and 'second'—demonstrates that Vatsyayana is thinking primarily in binary, more precisely dialectic, terms: two opposed terms modified by a third. (Vatsyayana actually

ii See chapter three, 'The Mythology of the *Kamasutra*'.

analogizes men and women to grammatical terms, in the discussion of gender stereotypes considered above, which does not take account of the third nature at all: 'By his physical nature, the man is the active agent [the subject] and the young woman is the passive locus [the locative case, in which the action takes place].'[22] [The object is the sexual act.])

But there is another, better reason why Vatsyayana uses the female pronoun for a person of the third nature, and that is because of her perceived gender: he lists the third nature among *women* who can be lovers.[23] This use of the pronoun 'she' can also be seen as an anticipation of the practices of some cross-dressing gay men of our day.

## SIR RICHARD BURTON ON THE 'THIRD NATURE'

The *Kamasutra* passage about people of the 'third nature' has been largely unknown outside Sanskrit circles because it was mistranslated in the version of the text that has been used by English-language readers (and, through translation, French readers) for over a century: the translation by Sir Richard Francis Burton, first published in 1883. Burton's translation misses the entire point about same-sex eroticism because he renders 'third nature' as 'eunuch' throughout. He also leaves out, entirely, the line that includes the 'third nature' in the list of women who are sexually available.[24] It would appear that he used the word 'eunuch' in its broader sense, to designate not a guardian in the harem but a man who had been castrated for one reason or another. Perhaps he confused the men of the third nature with *klibas*, the elastic category that includes both castrated men and homosexual men. Or with the Hijras, transvestites who were usually castrated, many of whom earn a living as male prostitutes in South Asia today, as they did during Burton's time, and are often called 'eunuchs'.[25] The Hijras, who have been part of South Asian society, but as marginal people, for centuries, do correspond rather closely to the first type of 'third nature', the cross-dressing female type that is dismissed after just a sentence or two in the *Kamasutra*, but not to the second type, the closeted male type, to which Vatsyayana devotes considerable attention.

Burton had written about the Hijras in the notes to his translation of the *Arabian Nights*, but there is no evidence of their existence at the time of the *Kamasutra*, nor is there anything about such a group in the *Kamasutra*. Why, then, did Burton use the word 'eunuch' to translate *tritiya prakrti*? Why did he not recognize the text's reference to sexually entire men who happened to prefer having (oral) sex with other men? Did he read the text as implying that this was the only option available to them due to some sort of genital malfunction? This cannot be the case, since Burton had undertaken at least one study of a male brothel (in Karachi)[26] staffed by 'boys and eunuchs'.[27] And his famous 'Terminal Essay' to the *Arabian Nights*, published in 1885, includes an 18,000-word essay entitled 'Pederasty' (later republished in his collection of essays entitled *The Erotic Traveller*) that was one of the first serious treatments of male homosexuality in English, though he stated that Hindus held the practice in abhorrence.[28] No, Burton's 'eunuchs' are, rather, the product of 'Orientalism': the depiction of 'Orientals' as simultaneously oversexed and feminized. The word 'eunuch' was frequently used in British writings about the Orient, conveying a vague sense of sexual excess, cruelty and impotence. Burton simply followed that tradition in his translation of the *Kamasutra*.

## SAME-SEX WOMEN

What about homoerotic women? Vatsyayana is unique in the literature of the period in describing lesbian activity. He does this at the beginning of the chapter about the harem, in a brief passage about what he calls 'Oriental customs'.[29] (The use of the term 'Oriental'—or 'Eastern' [*pracya*]—for what Vatsyayana regards as a disreputable lesbian practice in what was soon to be a colonized part of the Gupta Empire—indeed, the Eastern part—suggests that 'Orientalism' began not with the British but with the Orientals themselves.) These women use dildos, as well as bulbs, roots, or fruits that have the form of the male organ, and statues of men that have distinct sexual characteristics. But they engage in sexual acts with one another only in the absence of men, not through the kind of personal choice that drives a man of the third nature: 'The women of the harem cannot meet men, because they are carefully guarded; and since they have only one husband shared by many women in common, they are not satisfied. Therefore, they give pleasure to one another with the following techniques.'[30] Yashodhara's commentary helpfully suggests the particular vegetables that one might employ: 'By imagining a man, they experience a heightened emotion that gives extreme satisfaction. These things have a form just like the male sexual organ: the bulbs of arrow-root, plantain and so forth; the roots of coconut palms, bread fruit, and so forth; and the fruits of the bottle-gourd, cucumber, and so forth.' One can imagine little gardens of plantain and cucumber being cultivated within the inner rooms of the palace, the harem.

The *Kamasutra* makes only one brief reference to women who may have chosen women as sexual partners in preference to men: the text says that a girl may lose her virginity with a girlfriend or a servant girl, and the commentator specifies that 'They take her virginity by using a finger.'[31] Manu and Kautilya say that a woman who corrupts a virgin will be punished by having two of her fingers cut off[32]—a hint of what Manu and Kautilya—like Yashodhara—think lesbians do in bed. Vatsyayana never uses the verb 'to play the man's role' when he describes lesbian activities,[33] nor does he ever refer to women of this type as people of a 'third nature'. But the commentator's belief that the children produced when the woman is on top might be 'a little boy and little girl with reversed natures'[34] refers to the view that the 'reverse' intercourse of parents might wreak embryonic damage, resulting in the reversed gender behaviour of the third nature—significantly, for a girl as well as a boy, the *female* type not spelt out by the text's discussion of the 'third nature'.

## BISEXUALITY

In addition to male and female homosexual acts, there are a few oblique, passing remarks that suggest bisexuality. The female messenger may have had bisexual behaviour in mind when, praising the man's charm, she says, according to the commentator, 'He has such luck in love that he was desired even by a man.'[35] So, too, in the *Buddhacharita*,[36] composed in roughly the same period as the *Kamasutra*, the court chaplain encouraging a group of women to seduce the Buddha tells them, 'By your knowledge of the telltale signs of emotion, your flirtation, your perfect beauty, you are able to enflame the passion even of women, so how much more is this so of men?' In the *Kamasutra*, two verses embedded within the passage about fellatio performed by women describe men who engage in oral sex not by profession, like the men of the 'third nature', but out of love:

> Even young men, servants
> who wear polished earrings,
> indulge in oral sex
> only with certain men.
> And, in the same way, certain men-about-town
> who care for one another's welfare
> and have established trust
> do this service for one another.[37]

These men, who seem bound to one another by discriminating affection rather than promiscuous passion, are called 'men-about-town', *nagarakas*, the term used to designate the heterosexual heroes of the *Kamasutra*. In striking contrast with men of the third nature, always designated by the pronoun 'she', these men are described with nouns and pronouns that unambiguously designate males, yet they are grouped with women. Perhaps, then, they are bisexuals. The commentator on the *Kamasutra* even makes Dattaka,[iii] the author of the part of the text commissioned by the courtesans, a serial bisexual.[38]

Thus, despite the caution with which the text broaches

---

iii See chapter three, 'The Mythology of the *Kamasutra*'.

the topic of homosexuality, and even more cautiously, bisexuality, it is possible for us as readers to excavate several alternative sexualities latent in the text's somewhat fuzzy boundaries between homoeroticism and heteroeroticism. This sort of reading suggests various ways in which the *Kamasutra*'s implicit claim to sexual totality—everything anyone could ask to know about sex—might be opened out into a vision of gender infinity.

# 6

# THE MARE'S TRAP: THE NATURE AND CULTURE OF SEX[1]

We have noted the ways in which the *Kamasutra* veers between attitudes that strike the contemporary reader as reasonable and others that seem to find no parallels in the modern world.[i] One link between ancient India and the contemporary world is male anxiety about penis size, which remains a prevalent obsession on the Internet. And here again, as in so many of the other apparent parallels, we veer back and forth between conceptions of what is perceived as part of nature or part of culture.

## SIZE MATTERS

The passage describing genital size, and its significance, is placed at a critical moment at the very start of the part of the *Kamasutra* describing the sexual act:

> The man is called a 'hare', 'bull', or 'stallion', according to the size of his sexual organ; a woman, however, is called a 'doe', 'mare', or 'elephant cow'. And so there are three equal couplings, between sexual partners of similar size, and six unequal ones, between sexual partners of dissimilar size.[2]

Clearly the six paradigmatic animals are chosen for their size, and they do not match: a hare is smaller than a doe, a bull smaller than a mare, and a stallion smaller than an

---

i See chapter one, 'The Strange and the Familiar'.

elephant cow. (The elephant cow, the biggest, is the only animal to survive as a classificatory type in the much later *Kokashastra*, which speaks of four types of women: Lotus Woman [Padmini], Art Woman [Chitrini], Conch Woman [Shankhini], and Elephant Woman [Hastini]).

When the *Kamasutra* describes the possible positions, it uses these animal types as its basic referents for size. When the man is larger than the woman, the problem is relatively easily solved:

> At the moment of passion, in a coupling where the man is larger than the woman, a 'doe' positions herself in such a way as to stretch herself open inside. A 'doe' generally has three positions to choose from: the 'wide open', the 'yawning', or the 'Junoesque'.[3]

In addition, a 'doe' may use drugs to expand herself: 'An ointment made of powdered white lotus, blue lotus, "morningstar" tree blossoms, rose dammar blossoms, and marjoram makes a "doe" open wide.'[4]

But the 'doe' is the favoured woman, the ideal erotic partner; it is in other couplings, when the man is smaller than the woman, that male anxiety about phallic size raises its head, and the problems are not so easily resolved. The initial passage defining the three sizes continues: 'The equal couplings are the best, the one when the man is much larger or much smaller than the woman are the worst, and the rest are intermediate. Even in the medium ones, it is better for the man to be larger than the woman.'[5] Thus, there are two different, conflicting agendas set forth from the start: ideally, 'equal is best', but in fact the man has to be bigger, because women are by nature bigger: the biggest woman (the 'elephant cow') is much bigger than the biggest man (the 'stallion').

The text gives only relative, not absolute, sizes, but the commentary spells it out:

> The size of the penis is divided into the three categories of 'hare' and so forth, according to the length, in graduated order: six, nine, and twelve [fingers]. Its circumference should measure equal to its length. But some say, 'There is no fixed rule about the circumference.'[6]

The commentator is probably using the measurement of 'fingers', approximately ¾ of an inch each. The lengths therefore would be 4 ½", 6 ¾", and 9". Sir Richard Burton estimated lengths of 3", 4 ½", and 6", the latter 'of African or Negro dimensions'.[7] (We will simply note, in passing, the racist and Orientalist aspects of penis envy.) And that is why a man prefers a 'doe' to a 'mare' (let alone an 'elephant cow').

## THE PROBLEM OF DESIRE

The problem posed by the greater size of women is not easily solved, in part because it is not physical but mental. No proto-Kinsey went around in ancient India measuring the size of women's vulvas. It is a matter of fantasy, apparently a cross-cultural human fantasy, and it is not about physiology (for which there are physical correctives, as we will see) but about desire, the mare that no one has ever managed to tame, though so many have tried. And desire is affected not merely by size but by the other two criteria by which potential partners are ranked—duration and intensity of desire:

> A man has dull sexual energy if, at the time of making love, his enthusiasm is indifferent, his virility small, and he cannot bear to be wounded, and a man has average or fierce sexual energy in the opposite circumstances. The same goes for the woman. And so, just as with size, so with temperament, too, there are nine sorts of couplings. And similarly, with respect to endurance, men are quick, average, and long-lasting. Since there is no difference in the species of a couple, they seek a similar sensual pleasure. Therefore the woman should be treated in such a way that she achieves her sexual climax first. Since the similarity in climaxes has been proved in this way, there are nine forms of sex keyed to endurance, too, in terms of the time-to-climax, just as there are nine in terms of size and temperament.[8]

Why does Vatsyayana conclude from all of this that the woman should reach her climax first?[ii] The commentator explains:

> The best case is when the man and woman achieve their sexual pleasure at the same time, because that is an equal coupling. But if it does not happen at the same time, and the man reaches his climax first, his banner is no longer at full mast, and the woman does not reach her climax. Therefore, if the coupling is unequal rather than equal, the woman should be treated with kisses, embraces, and so forth, in such a way that she achieves her sexual pleasure first. When the woman reaches her climax first, the man, remaining inside her, puts on speed and reaches his own climax.[9]

---

ii A concern that we have already noted in chapter four, 'Women in the *Kamasutra*'.

For the problem of fit is merely one aspect of the greater problem of satisfaction. That is why the commentator assures us, speaking of the woman who has the most sexual energy (of three types) and lasts longest (also of three types): 'The passion even of a long-lasting woman whose sexual energy is fierce is quelled when she is slapped.' The physical violence that we have already noted as a characteristic of the Kautilyan *Kamasutra*[iii] is here given at least a partial explanation: it is necessary to deal with oversized women.

Just as mares are bigger than hares, the logic goes, so, as the commentator points out in the context of an argument about female orgasm, women have far more desire than men: 'Women want a climax that takes a long time to produce, because their desire is eight times that of a man. Given these conditions, it is perfectly right to say that "a fair-eyed woman cannot be sated by men", because men's desire is just one eighth of women's.'[10] Here he is quoting a well-known Sanskrit saying: 'A fire is never sated by any amount of logs, nor the ocean by the rivers that flow into it; death cannot be sated by all the creatures in the world, nor a fair-eyed woman by any amount of men.'

The double knowledge of bisexuals such as Dattaka[iv] is matched by the special expertise of serial androgynes such as the female-to-male bisexual Chudala, who says, when she is a woman, that a woman has eight times as much pleasure (kama) as a man, which could also be translated as eight times as much desire.[11] Yashodhara may well have this mythology in mind when, commenting

iii See chapter two, 'The Kautilyan *Kamasutra*'.

iv See chapter five, 'The Third Nature'.

on Vatsyayana's remark that 'It is commonly said: "The man runs out of fluid before the woman runs out of fluid,"'[12] he explains, 'He runs out of fluids first because the woman has eight times as much fluid as a man,' and then repeats the saying he cited just a few verses earlier: 'And so it is commonly said: "A fair-eyed woman cannot be sated by men."'[13]

Women are also bigger in the sense that their sexuality is bigger; they are harder to satisfy than men are. This is the argument put forth by one of the 'scholars' of the erotic science with whom Vatsyayana disagrees, in this case on the question of whether women have orgasms:[v]

> A woman has an itch, which the man, during sex, scratches continually. And when this scratching is combined, in addition, with the sensual pleasure of erotic arousal, it produces a different feeling, and this is what she thinks of as sensual pleasure. The scratching of an itch also feels good for a long time. Because of this, women love the man whose sexual energy lasts for a long time, but they resent a man whose sexual energy ends quickly.[14]

This is taken as one of the proofs that women do indeed have orgasms—if a man can last long enough. The 'grinding down' position, in which the woman bends her thighs so close to her chest that the man enters her from below, is particularly effective for the relieving of that itch, as the commentator points out: 'He thrusts from below into the lower part of her vagina, violently, because the itch is most extensive in the lower part of the vagina.'[15]

---

v See chapter four, 'Women in the *Kamasutra*'.

## POSITIONAL SOLUTIONS

Size is still an essential part of this formula, for reasons that the commentary (on the verse that says 'It is better for the man to be larger than the woman') spells out:

> In the coupling when the man is much larger [a 'stallion' with a 'doe'], a woman's itch is most satisfactorily relieved; she accommodates the large penis inside her by assuming a position such as the 'wide open', stretching her vagina. But in the coupling when the man is much smaller [a 'hare' with an 'elephant cow'], even when she contracts her vagina by assuming a position such as the 'cup', there is no relief for her. Vatsyayana will speak later about ways of changing the size of the sexual organ, in which the woman stretches hers and the man uses devices to increase his. But it is said: 'If a lover has a small penis, no matter how long the man works, women, they say, do not grow very fond of him, because he does not relieve their itch.' And the saying is right.[16]

We have already seen Vatsyayana warn that a woman who is not satisfied may leave her husband.[vi] Again, there is the implicit threat that a woman who 'do[es] not grow very fond of' a man who is not well-endowed may leave him.

But the *Kamasutra* had its ways of coping with satisfaction, a kind of end-run around the obstacle of size, to which the commentator here alludes; for, the *Kamasutra* assures us, 'In a coupling where the man is smaller, an "elephant cow" contracts herself inside.'[17]

---

vi See chapter four, 'Women in the *Kamasutra*'.

## MECHANICAL AND PHARMACEUTICAL SOLUTIONS

And if the positions do not solve the problem, one can always resort to sex tools, drugs, and, in final desperation, surgery. The *Kamasutra* helpfully remarks, 'If you are unable to pleasure a woman of fierce sexual energy, have recourse to devices,'[18] and provides an extensive collection of methods to increase and enhance the size of the penis, a combination of dildos, drugs and surgical procedures. We have noted the use of sex tools between women in the harem;[vii] they are also useful in heterosexual encounters. When the man is smaller than the woman, Vatsyayana drily comments, 'Sex tools may also be used.'[19] (The commentator clarifies, 'If he is larger than she is, there is no need for sex tools.')

The 'elephant cow' may use drugs to contract: 'An ointment made of the white flowers of the "cuckoo's-eye" caper bush makes an "elephant-cow" contract tightly for one night.'[20] But drugs may have more extensive sexual powers:

> If you make a powder by pulverizing leaves scattered by the wind, garlands left over from corpses, and peacocks' bones, or pulverize a female 'circle-maker' buzzard that died a natural death, and mix the powder with honey and gooseberry, it puts someone in your power. If you mix the same powder with monkey shit and scatter the mixture over a virgin, she will not be given to another man.[21]

Or:

> If you coat your penis with an ointment made with powdered white thorn-apple, black pepper, and long

vii See chapter five, 'The Third Nature'.

> pepper, mixed with honey, you put your sexual partner in your power. If you pulverize a female 'circle-maker' buzzard that died a natural death, and mix the powder with honey and gooseberry; or if you cut the knotty roots of the milkwort and milk-hedge plants into pieces, coat them with a powder of red arsenic and sulfur, dry and pulverize the mixture seven times, mix it with honey, and spread it on your penis, you put your sexual partner in your power.[22]

And so on. The commentator's comment on this ('Do this in such a way that the woman you want does not realize, "A man with something spread on his penis is making love to me"') has inspired at least one reader to remark, 'Any woman who would let you make love to her with all that stuff smeared on you would have to be madly in love with you already.'[23]

But if drugs fail, the recommended surgery is fairly brutal:

> The people of the South pierce a boy's penis just like his ears. A young man has it cut with a knife and then stands in water as long as the blood flows. To keep the opening clear, he has sexual intercourse that very night, continuously. Then, after an interval of one day, he cleans the opening with astringent decoctions. He enlarges it by putting larger and larger spears of reeds and ivory-tree wood in it, and he cleans it with a piece of sugar-cane coated with honey. After that, he enlarges it by inserting a tube of lead with a protruding knot on the end, and he lubricates it with the oil of the marking-nut. He inserts into the enlarged opening sex tools made in various shapes. They must be able to bear a lot of use, and may be soft or rough according to individual preferences.[24]

Well, if that doesn't work, try this:

> Rub your penis with the bristles of insects born in trees, then massage it with oil for ten nights, then rub it again and massage it again. When it swells up as the result of this treatment, lie down on a cot with your face down and let your penis hang down from a hole in the cot. Then you may assuage the pain with cool astringents and, by stages, finish the treatment. This swelling, which lasts for a lifetime, is the one that voluptuaries call 'prickled'.[25]

Granted, I have chosen extreme surgical examples, but the pharmaceutical recommendations, though less grotesque, seem hardly more practical. Nevertheless, they are guaranteed to work.

At this point, it might seem that ancient India had come to terms with what Freud called penis envy (and Woody Allen pointed out was more of a problem for boys than for girls). Perhaps size does not matter after all? But inadequate size turns out to be just the tip of the iceberg of the problem of sexuality in the *Kamasutra*.

## THE MARE'S TRAP

A counterweight to the problem of desire is the problem of vulnerability. It turns out that a man may be caught between the Scylla of a woman who is too big, producing a kind of sexual agoraphobia, and the Charybdis of a woman who is too small, inspiring a kind of sexual claustrophobia.

The position overwhelmingly favoured in illustrations of the *Kamasutra* is the one that the *Kamasutra* advises a man to use when the woman's genitals are much smaller than those of the man, the ideal combination of 'doe' and 'stallion'.[26] The *Kamasutra* describes three variants:

> Her head thrown down, her pelvis raised up, she is 'wide open'. Without lowering her thighs, suspending them while spreading them wide apart, she receives him in the 'yawning' position. Parting her thighs around his sides, at the same time she pulls her knees back around her own sides, in the 'Junoesque' position, which can only be done with practice.[27]

What I have called 'Junoesque' is literally 'of Indrani', the wife of the god Indra.[viii]

But this position recommended for the 'doe', the 'Junoesque' position, turns out to be rather dangerous: 'Her head thrown down, her pelvis raised up, she is "wide open". This position must allow a way for the man to slide back.'[28] And the commentator warns:

> When she is making love with the man's penis inside her, she should slide back with her hips; or when the man is making love with her he should slide back little by little, so that they do not press together too tightly. For if he moves inside her too roughly, she can be injured, and the man's foreskin can be torn off, which physicians call 'ruptured foreskin'.[29]

So the small woman may be too small.

But it gets worse: the too-large woman may also be too small, by overcompensating, as it were, for her size. The 'elephant cow' is encouraged to employ a sexual position that catapults her unsuspecting partner from the frying pan of insatiable enormity to the fire of strangulating tightness. It begins, disarmingly, with the harmless missionary position:

---

viii See chapter three, 'The Mythology of the *Kamasutra*'.

> Both partners stretch out both of their two legs straight. If, as soon as he has penetrated her, he squeezes her two thighs together tightly, it becomes the 'squeeze'. If she then crosses her thighs, it becomes the 'circle'. In the 'mare's trap', which can only be done with practice, she grasps him, like a mare, so tightly that he cannot move.[30]

There is also a variation with the woman on top: 'When she grasps him in the "mare's trap" position and draws him more deeply into her or contracts around him and holds him there for a long time, that is the "tongs"',[31] and the commentator explains: 'She uses the lips of the vagina as a tongs.'

This is the only sexual position that the *Kamasutra* associates with a mare (it is called Carezza or Pompoir in Europe), and, confusingly, it is reserved for the 'elephant cow' rather than the 'mare' woman. The confusion arises because the horse, hyper-sexualized, is the only animal that appears on both the male and the female sides of the initial triads of men and women, and the male and female equines are not paired; the stallion is the largest male, while the mare is merely the middle-sized woman.[32] Yet, in Hindu mythology, the mare is regarded as sexually dangerous, bursting with repressed violence: the doomsday fire is lodged in the mouth of a mare who wanders on the floor of the ocean, waiting for the moment when she will be released, to burn everything to ashes.[33] The mare is the sexual animal par excellence; the commentator on the *Kamasutra*, glossing the phrase 'two people of the same species' (in the argument that women have the same sort of climax as men[ix]) offers

ix See chapter four, 'Women in the *Kamasutra*'.

this example, surely not at random: 'Two people of different species, such as a man and a mare, would have different kinds of sensual pleasure; and so he specifies the same species, the human species.'[34]

The conflation, in an animal image, of the woman who is too big with the image of the woman who traps you (and is, in that sense, too small) begins in ancient India in a text from about 900 BCE:

> Long-tongue was a demoness who had vaginas on every limb of her body. To subdue her, the god Indra equipped his grandson with penises on every limb and sent him to her. As soon as he had his way with her, he remained firmly stuck in her; Indra then ran at her and struck her down with his thunderbolt.[35]

Long-tongue is a dog, and she and Indra's grandson get stuck together as dogs sometimes do; in this case, it spells her death, not his, but clearly it is an image of excess that corresponds to her excessively numerous vaginas, each one presumably demanding to be satisfied. So this is the Catch-22: if the woman is too big you cannot satisfy her, but if she is too small (*or* too big), you may be injured and/or trapped inside her.

## ANIMALS AND HUMANS: NATURE AND CULTURE

The tendency to identify women, more than men, as animals is assumed in a passage that makes them, in contrast with men, creatures both explicitly likened to animals and said to speak a meaningless animal language:

> There are eight kinds of screaming: whimpering, groaning, babbling, crying, panting, shrieking, or sobbing. And there

> are various sounds that have meaning, such as 'Mother!', 'Stop!' , 'Let go!', 'Enough!' As a major part of moaning she may use, according to her imagination, the cries of the dove, cuckoo, green pigeon, parrot, bee, nightingale, goose, duck, and partridge. He strikes her on her back with his fist when she is seated on his lap. Then she pretends to be unable to bear it and beats him in return, while groaning, crying, or babbling. If she protests, he strikes her on the head until she sobs, using a hand whose fingers are slightly bent, which is called the 'out-stretched hand'. At this she babbles with sounds inside her mouth, and she sobs. When the sex ends, there is panting and crying. Shrieking is a sound like a bamboo splitting, and sobbing sounds like a berry falling into water. Always, if a man tries to force his kisses and so forth on her, she moans and does the very same thing back to him. When a man in the throes of passion slaps a woman repeatedly, she uses words like 'Stop!' or 'Let me go!' or 'Enough!' or 'Mother!' and utters screams mixed with laboured breathing, panting, crying, and groaning. As passion nears its end, he beats her extremely quickly, until the climax. At this, she begins to babble, fast, like a partridge or a goose. Those are the ways of groaning and slapping.[36]

It is worth noting that these women make the noises of birds, never of mammals, let alone the mammals that characterize the three paradigmatic sizes of women. Moreover, one of the birds whose babbling the sexual woman imitates—the parrot—appears elsewhere in the *Kamasutra* as one of the two birds who can be taught to speak like humans: teaching parrots and mynah birds to talk is a skill that both a man and a woman should learn, and that a man can use to lure a woman to his home (the ancient Indian equivalent of coming up to see his etchings).[37] The passage about slapping and groaning inculcates, as we have noted before, what we now recognize as the rape mentality, disregarding a woman's protests against rape.[x] And this treatment of women is justified by a combination of the official naming of women after over-sized animals and the expectation that in the throes of passion women will speak like animals.

The practice of naming the sexual movements after animals—the 'boar's thrust', the 'bull's thrust', 'frolicking like a sparrow'[38]—has inspired European satires like this parodied protest on behalf of animal rights: 'When the lovers decide to join in any of the Animal Embraces such as the Bull Elephant embrace, the Howler Monkey embrace, The Vulture Has Second Thoughts, The Mule Escapes Exploitation, and The Antelopes Form a Support Group, they…call into question the very idea of using animal names to describe human sexual activities.'[39] The animal imagery implies that there is a very basic sense in which sex, even when done according to the book, as it were, is bestial.

Clearly the six paradigmatic animals are chosen for their size, but the dissymmetry in their sizes reveals that they have not literal but symbolic implications for the relationship between men and women. Vatsyayana almost certainly inherited from his predecessors, as well as from the broader ancient Indian tradition, the animals, the mares and hares, as well as the male anxiety and the positional nomenclature as a whole. But the *Kamasutra*'s claim to fame is precisely its boast that it has found ways—positions, tools, drugs—to

---

x See chapter four, 'Women in the *Kamasutra*'.

deal with the mind as well as the body, to satisfy women not only of any size but of any degree of desire. (There is an American expression for this approach: it is not the size of the wand, but its magic.) Vatsyayana's words do not seem to reflect male anxiety at all; the women are depicted not as enormous monsters but as pliant and manipulatable sources of great pleasure.

And this is because the book insists that the sexuality of animals is different from that of humans. Despite its recurrent zoological terminology, the *Kamasutra* argues that people are not animals, and that human men and women have resources that animals lack. The very passages in which people are advised, for the sake of variety, to imitate the sexual behaviour of animals, or women are told to imitate the cries of animals, imply that such behaviour is therefore, by definition, different from ours. Vivé la différence: because we are not animals, we can use culture, more precisely the technique of the *Kamasutra*, to overcome our baser instincts, which must surely incline male phallic anxiety.

Vatsyayana distinguishes human sexuality from animal sexuality in the argument that he puts forward at the very beginning to justify his text:

> Scholars say: 'Since even animals manage sex by themselves, and since it goes on all the time, it should not have to be handled with the help of a text.' Vatsyayana says: Because a man and a woman depend upon one another in sex, it requires a method, and this method is learnt from the *Kamasutra*. The mating of animals, by contrast, is not based upon any method, because they are not fenced in, they mate only when the females are in their fertile season and until they achieve their goal, and they act without thinking about it first.[40]

Yashodhara's commentary expands upon these ideas:

> Even animals like cows, whose intellects are shrouded in torpor, visibly manage sex without instruction from a textbook; how much more must this happen among humans, whose intellects consist primarily of passion? As it is said:
>
> For desire is satisfied without instruction,
> and does not have to be taught.
> Who is the guru for deer and birds, for the methodology
> to give and take pleasure with those they desire?
>
> And desire goes on all the time, because the qualities of wanting and hating are always there in the soul. There is no guarding or any other form of concealment, because the females of the species are loose. Animals mate only during their fertile season. Humans who want children, however, do it during a woman's fertile season but also outside her fertile season, in order to enjoy and please the woman. So animals and humans are not the same. And animals engage in sex just until they achieve a climax; they do not wonder, 'Has he reached his climax or not?' and therefore wish to mate a second time. And so, since the goal of animals and humans is not the same, animals need no method for sex. Animals, moreover, do not first think, before engaging in sex, 'What will happen to dharma, artha, sons, relatives, and the prosperity of our faction?' Sex just happens to animals in their own way.

Humans, whose sexuality is more complex than that of animals, are more repressed—'fenced in', as the text puts it. Humans, therefore, have a different sexuality from animals, and need a text for it, where animals do not. Humans also have, unlike animals, the capacity for culture.

## THE CULTURE OF THE *KAMASUTRA*

The privilege of the *Kamasutra* lovers is expressed in the opulence of the instructions on the home decorating of the two bedrooms in the home of the ideal lover.[xi] The two bedrooms are not, as in European conventions, a hint that the man and woman may not be sleeping together; au contraire, as the commentary makes clear:

> The inner bedroom is where the wives sleep. The outer bedroom is for sex. The couch is for the man to sleep on after sex. That is what decent people do; but the lovers of courtesans sleep together with them in the bedroom, and have no need for a couch. And so there is a saying:
>
> 'The lover makes love with his beloved
> wherever he happens to be,
> but a wise man, a pure man,
> does not sleep there on that polluted bed.'[41]

Many other items are also strewn around the bedrooms—lemon bark and books, for instance—and the commentary tells us why they are necessary:

> The lemon bark is chewed to dispel the bad taste in the mouth and prevent bad breath; about this there is a saying:
> 'The lover who, in the evening, sucks
> a stick of lemon bark, smeared with honey,
> is not plagued by foul breath
> when he is caught in the net of his woman's arms.'
> The book is understood to be a book of recent poetry, to read aloud.[42]

---

xi See chapter two, 'The Kautilyan *Kamasutra*'.

When the man receives the woman, we learn more about his preparations:

> In a room of his house dedicated to sex, a room decorated, full of flowers, and fragrant with perfume and incense, the man-about-town receives the woman, when she has bathed and adorned herself and has drunk the proper amount; he puts her at ease and offers her another drink. He sits down on her right side and touches her hair, the fringe of her sari, and the knot of her waistband. He embraces her gently with his left arm to prepare to make love. They talk together about things that they have done together before, joking and titillating, touching upon all sorts of things hidden and obscene. Then there may be singing and instrumental music, with or without dancing, and conversation about the fine arts, and then he entices her with another drink.[43]

There are also things to eat and drink:

> Both of them may drink some water or eat some bite-sized snacks or something else, according to their temperament and inclination: fruit juice, grilled foods, sour rice-broth, soups with small pieces of roasted meats, mangoes, dried meat, citrus fruits with sugar, according to the tastes of the region. As he tastes each one he tells her, 'This one is sweet' or 'delicate' or 'soft' and offers it to her.[44]

But we must not assume that this bedroom is inside the house. In a hot climate like India's, many people sleep on the tops of buildings, the rich in often spectacular penthouse gardens. The *Kamasutra* describes the roof as a place not primarily on which to make love but one to go to after love-making:

> As for the end of sex, when their passion has ebbed, the man and woman go out separately to the bathing place, embarrassed, not looking at one another, as if they were not even acquainted with one another. When they return, they sit down in their usual places without embarrassment, and chew some betel, and he himself rubs sandalwood paste or some other scented oil on her body. He embraces her with his left arm and, holding a cup in his hand, persuades her to drink. Sometimes they sit on the rooftop porch to enjoy the moonlight, and tell stories that suit their mood. As she lies in his lap, looking at the moon, he points out the rows of the constellations to her; they look at the Pleiades, the Pole Star, and the garland of Seven Sages that form the Great Bear. That is the end of sex. They look at the circle of the moon with eyes moist and flickering with passion. They talk about it all, about the desires they felt when they first saw one another long ago, and the unhappiness they felt when they were later separated. And when they finish talking they embrace and kiss with passion. Through these and other feelings the young couple's passion grows again.[45]

And we may assume that, when the passion had, in fact, grown again, they stayed on the roof.

In this way, the *Kamasutra* offers a solution to the problem of the violence of sexuality that it inherited, in part, from the *Arthashastra*.[xii] Culture—the unique culture of ancient India—is the answer to the universal and perhaps natural problem of sexuality anxiety. But this solution was available only to the privileged few, and, as we will see,[xiii] it was trumped by other forces in the later history of India.

---

xii See chapter two, 'The Kautilyan *Kamasutra*'.

xiii See chapter seven, 'From Kama to Karma'.

# 7

# THE RISE AND FALL OF KAMA AND THE *KAMASUTRA*[1]

## KAMA IN THE EARLY HISTORY OF INDIA

Kama is as old as Hinduism. The earliest Hindu text, the *Rig Veda* (c. 1500 BCE), revels in the language of both pleasure and fertility and tells us that kama, desire, came upon the creator as the first seed of mind at the very beginning of creation.[2] The Upanishads, which followed a few centuries later, analogized the Vedic oblation of butter into the sacrificial fire to the act of sexual procreation: the worshipper in a sexual embrace with his wife imagines each part of the act as a part of the ritual of the oblation: the firewood is the vulva; the smoke, the pubic hair; the flame, the vagina; and the embers and sparks are the acts of penetration and climax.[3] Presumably anyone making the offering into the fire could also imagine each action as its sexual parallel. This is a very early instance of the interpretation of human sexual matters in terms of non-sexual, sacred matters (or, if you prefer, the reverse). Sensuality continued to keep its foot in the door of the house of religion throughout the history of India.

But the Upanishads also introduced into India the concept of two paths, one the path of family life, society and children, the other the path of renunciation, solitary meditation and asceticism. The tension between the two paths, the violent (sacrificial), materialistic, sensual and potentially addictive path of worldliness on the one hand, and the non-violent (vegetarian), ascetic, spiritual and controlled path of renunciation, on the other, was sometimes expressed as the balance between bourgeois householders and homeless seekers, or between traditions that regarded karma—the accumulated record of good and bad deeds—as a good or a bad thing, respectively.

The tension remains in the Tantras, a large body of texts, composed between about 650 and 1800 CE, which proposed strikingly transgressive ritual actions, violating all the taboos of conventional Hinduism, such as drinking wine and menstrual blood, eating meat and engaging in sexual activity with forbidden women. These Tantras thus collapsed the Upanishadic metaphor, saying that the ritual sexual act is not just *like* a ritual (as it is in the Upanishads) but is itself a ritual, the equivalent of making an offering into the fire. Other Tantras, however, situated within the anti-erotic tradition of Hinduism, insisted that the ritual instructions were never intended to be followed literally, but were purely symbolic. They argued that 'wine' really meant a meditational nectar, that 'flesh' meant the tongue of the practitioner, and that the sexual act stood for 'the supreme essence.'[4] This was a very early form of censorship, and a very mild form, for it merely proposed an alternative, anti-erotic interpretation of the text but did not attempt to muzzle the other, erotic interpretation.

And so the two paths of meditation and ritual action lived side by side, sometimes coexisting in a single worshipper, sometimes within a group, as, for instance, in some texts that say that beginners actually do the Tantric ritual, while advanced practitioners just meditate. The split-level connotations were present from the start. Given the attention that Indian literary theory pays to double meanings, to words and indeed whole literary works that simultaneously mean two different things[5]—the 'Century' of the poet Amaru consists of a hundred poems that are simultaneously erotic and ascetic—it seems wise to assume that the Tantrics were capable of walking and chewing imaginary gum at the same time.

Kama continued to thrive in Hinduism. Many poems to gods in the medieval devotional tradition of bhakti imagine the god as a lover, often an unfaithful lover, and depict the relationship with all the sensual details of good erotic poetry. The poet Kshetrayya, who may have lived in the mid-seventeenth century, and who worshipped a form of the god Krishna, imagined a courtesan speaking to her customer who is both her lover and her god. Kshetrayya's songs survived among courtesans and were performed by male Brahmin dancers who played female roles. His poems speak of such down-to-earth matters as a woman's concern to find a drug or a magic potion to abort the child that she conceived from her lover—the god and her customer.[6]

In addition to these religious texts that incorporated eroticism, there were more worldly texts that treated the erotic *tout court*, of which the *Kamasutra* is the most famous.The *Kamasutra*'s ideas about gender are surprisingly modern, as we have already seen,[i] and its stereotypes of feminine and masculine natures are unexpectedly subtle. It also reveals attitudes to women's education and sexual freedom, and non-judgmental views of homosexual acts, that are strikingly more liberal than those of other texts in ancient India—or, in many cases, contemporary India. The

---

i See chapter five, 'The Third Nature'.

*Kamasutra* was a revolutionary document for sexually liminal people, and for women. It exerted a profound influence on subsequent Indian literature, particularly in court life and in the privileged, classless society that it describes at great length. But, at the same time, the dharma texts like Manu's *dharmashastra*, with their deep suspicion of women and eroticism, retained their stranglehold on much of Hindu society. And then came the British.

## DETUMESCENCE UNDER THE BRITISH

A Supreme Court ruling from 1862 states that 'Krishna...the love hero, the husband of 16,000 princesses...tinges the whole system (of Hinduism) with the strain of carnal sensualism, of strange, transcendental lewdness.'[7] Given this view of everyday Hinduism, it is hardly surprising that Evangelical Protestants greatly preferred the other path of Hinduism, the philosophical, renunciant path.

Influenced by British Protestantism, and embarrassed by aspects of their faith that the colonial rulers found abhorrent or ridiculous, the highly Anglicized Indian elite during the Raj developed new forms of Hinduism, particularly the movement known as the Bengal Renaissance or the Hindu Renaissance. (There is some irony in the fact that Bengal was also the place that nourished Tantra and the erotic tradition of the loves of Krishna and Radha.) Following the British lead, these Hindus largely wrote off the dominant strain of Hinduism that celebrated the passions of the gods. Eventually, these movements grew into the form of Neo-Vedanta called Sanatana Dharma (Eternal or Universal Dharma) that is embraced by many Hindus to this day. Sanatana Dharma is the banner of Hindutva, the fundamentalist, nationalist branch of Hinduism that, in most cases, presides over the censorship of art, film, literature and social behaviour.

The British lion, even after its official death in India in 1947, dealt another blow to Indian freedom of expression through the Film Censor Board, which, from the early 1950s, implemented a policy basis that had roots among the British (who had worried more about sedition than about sex). The Film Censor Board's concern for visual pedagogy, nationalism and publicity cast a shadow that extended over Indian visual arts and literature as well as film.

In the nineteenth and twentieth centuries, liberal Indian intellectuals, who noticed the shift in attitudes to Hinduism's erotic past from appreciation to embarrassment, tended to explain contemporary Hindu prudery in terms of power and patronage from the past. As James McConnachie summarized the situation, 'Erotic literature had been the creation of poets and princes, the argument ran, and as "lascivious" Hindu despots had given way to "fanatical" Mughal overlords, the patronage on which erotic literature depended had withered and died.'[8] V.S. Naipaul in his book *Half a Life* offers his own, rather jaded, version of this accusation:

> ...[I]n our culture there is no seduction. Our marriages are arranged. There is no art of sex. Some of the boys here talk to me of the *Kama Sutra*. Nobody talked about that at home. It was an upper-caste text, but I don't believe my poor father, brahmin though he is, ever looked at a copy. That philosophical-practical way of dealing with sex belongs to our past, and that world was ravaged and destroyed by the Muslims.[9]

And then (the twisted, chauvinist argument goes) came the British missionaries, adding insult to injury. Thus nationalists blamed India's sexual conservatism on 'an unholy combination of imposed Muslim religiosity and imported British "Victorianism"'.[10]

There is some truth in that general historical argument, but it has three serious flaws. First, as for the Muslims, it ignores the enthusiasm for the erotic arts on the part of such Muslims as the Lodi dynasty in the sixteenth century, who commissioned one of the last great works of Sanskrit eroticism, the *Ananga Ranga*,[11] and the Mughals (particularly Akbar and Dara Shikoh) who had textbooks of Hindu erotic arts and religious texts translated from Sanskrit to Persian and illustrated with Persian painting techniques. The Nationalists dismissed all of this, ungenerously, as 'the last, valedictory flourishing of a tragically deracinated tradition'. Second, blaming the British for Hindu prudery allows the very real memory of missionary Puritanism and the racist snobbery of the Raj club culture to overpower the equally important role of other sorts of Brits in the rediscovery of India's erotic heritage.[12] Most of all, blaming the Muslims and the British ignores the history of native Hindu anti-eroticism. For, as we have seen,[ii] India had its own home-grown traditions of prudery in opposition to its own sensuality.

## SIR RICHARD BURTON'S VERSION OF THE *KAMASUTRA*

One reason why the *Kamasutra* plays almost no role at all in the sexual consciousness of contemporary Indians is that it

ii See chapter two, 'The Kautilyan *Kamasutra*'.

is known, in both India and Europe, almost entirely through the flawed English translation by Sir Richard Francis Burton. (Popular, abridged versions of the *Kamasutra* in Hindi and other Indian languages have also often used Burton's English translation, rather than the original Sanskrit, as the source). This translation was published in 1883, a time when the Hindus, cowering under the scorn of the Protestant proselytizers, wanted to sweep the *Kamasutra* under the Upanishadic rug. The journalist Curt Gentry, writing in the *San Francisco Chronicle* at that time, suggested that the publication of Burton's *Kamasutra* translation 'might act as a useful corrective to the prevailing cliché of India as a land of asceticism'.[13] And in many ways, it did. Burton did for the *Kamasutra* what Max Müller did for the *Rig Veda* during this same period; his translation had a profound effect upon literature across Europe and America. But it did not bring the sexual freedom of the *Kamasutra* into Hindu consciousness.

Victorian British attitudes to Hindu eroticism ricocheted between the pornographers and the prudes, and Burton, a connoisseur of eroticism in Arabic as well as Indian culture, was certainly not a prude. His main contribution was the courage and determination to publish the work at all; he was the Larry Flynt of his day. To get around the censorship laws, Burton set up an imaginary publishing house, The Kama Shastra Society of London and Benares, with printers said to be in Benares or Cosmopoli. (The title page read: 'The Kama Sutra of Vatsyayana, Translated from the Sanscrit. In Seven Parts, with Preface, Introduction and Concluding Remarks. Cosmopoli: 1883: for the Kama Shastra Society of London and Benares, and for private circulation only.')

Even though it was not legally published in England and the United States until 1962, the Burton *Kamasutra* soon after its publication in 1883 became 'one of the most pirated books in the English language', constantly reprinted, often with a new preface to justify the new edition, sometimes without any attribution to Burton.[14]

This lack of attribution is actually quite appropriate, for the Burton translation is not primarily the work of Burton. It was far more the work of Forster Fitzgerald ('Bunny') Arbuthnot, whose name appears on the title page with Burton's only in some editions, though Burton later referred to the *Kamasutra* translation as 'Arbuthnot's Vatsyayana'.[15] In fact, the translation owed even more to two Indian scholars whose names do not appear on the title page at all: Bhagavanlal Indrajit and Shivaram Parashuram Bhide. (There is a pre-post-colonial irony in the fact that Arbuthnot later tried to get the censors off his trail by stating, in 1885, a half-truth that he almost certainly regarded as a lie: that the translation was done entirely by Indian pundits.)[16] It really should, therefore, be known as the Indrajit-Bhide-Arbuthnot-Burton translation, but since Burton was by far the most famous member of the team, it has always been called the Burton translation.

In many ways, it should be called the Burton mistranslation. For, in crucial passages, the Sanskrit text simply does not say what Burton (or perhaps one of the Indian pundits who really did the work) says it says. The Burton translation robs women of their voices, turning direct quotes into indirect quotes, thus losing the force of the dialogue that animates the work and erasing the vivid presence of the many women who speak in the *Kamasutra*, replacing these voices with reported speech rephrased by a man. Thus, where the text says that, when a man is striking a woman,[iii] 'She uses words like "Stop!" or "Let me go!" or "Enough!" or "Mother!"'[17] Burton translates it like this: 'She continually utters words expressive of prohibition, sufficiency, or desire of liberation.' Moreover, when the text says that this may happen 'When a man [is] in the throes of passion', and 'If a man tries to force his kisses and so forth on her', Burton says it happens 'When the woman is not accustomed to striking', reversing the genders and reversing the point.[18]

Burton also erodes women's agency by mistranslating or erasing some passages in which women have strong privileges.[iv] Take this passage (here translated more or less literally) about a wife's powers of recrimination:

> Mildly offended by the man's infidelities, she does not accuse him too much, but she scolds him with abusive language when he is alone or among friends. She does not, however, use love-sorcery worked with roots, for, Gonardiya says, 'Nothing destroys trust like that.'[19]

Burton renders it:

> In the event of any misconduct on the part of her husband, she should not blame him excessively, though she be a little displeased. She should not use abusive language toward him, but rebuke him with conciliatory words, whether he be in the company of friends or alone. Moreover, she

iii See chapter two, 'The Kautilyan *Kamasutra*', and chapter six, 'The Mare's Trap'.

iv See chapter four, 'Women in the *Kamasutra*'.

> should not be a scold, for, says Gonardiya, 'There is no cause of dislike on the part of a husband so great as this characteristic in a wife'.[20]

What is wrong with this picture? In the first place, Burton mistranslated the word for 'love-sorcery worked with roots' (*mulakarika*), which he renders as 'she should not be a scold' (though elsewhere he correctly translates *mulakarika*). Second, 'misconduct' is not so much a mistranslation as an error of judgment, for the word in question (*apacara*) does have the general meaning of 'misconduct', but in an erotic context it takes on the more specific meaning of 'infidelity', a choice that is supported by the remedy that the text suggests (and rejects): love-magic. But the most serious problem is the word 'not' that Burton gratuitously adds and that negates the wife's right to use abusive language against her straying husband, a denial only somewhat qualified by the added phrase, that she might 'rebuke him with conciliatory words'. Was this an innocent error or does it reflect a sexist bias? We cannot know. An even more serious disservice to the *Kamasutra* was done by Burton's mistranslation of the passages about people of the 'third nature'.[v]

The so-called Burton translation is widely read in Europe and America. It is free (at first poached from the illegal editions, then long out of copyright) and recognizable as what people think the *Kamasutra* should be. Indeed, it is quite a wonderful text: great fun to read, extraordinarily bold and frank for its time, and in many places a fairly approximate representation of the Sanskrit original. It

---

v See chapter five, 'The Third Nature'.

remains precious, like Edward Fitzgerald's *Rubaiyat*, as a monument of English literature, but it is certainly not a monument of Indian literature.

## THE DEMISE OF KAMA

An adolescent girl in Vikram Chandra's story 'Kama' says, 'Sister Carmina didn't want to tell us. It's the *Kama Sutra*, which she says isn't in the library. But Gisela's parents have a copy which they think is hidden away on the top of their shelf. We looked it up there.' And the adult to whom she tells this says, 'You put that book back where you found it. And don't read any more.'[21] In India today, urban, affluent, usually anglophone people will give a copy of the *Kamasutra* (in English translation) as a wedding present, to demonstrate their open-mindedness and sophistication, but most people will merely sneak a surreptitious look at it in someone else's house.

A pervasive and often violent moral policing has taken over parts of the Indian world today. A typical instance of this occurred in 2007, when a twenty-three-year-old student of Fine Arts at Baroda University named Chandramohan Srilamantula mounted an exhibition for other students and staff. He had previously received awards for his work, including the Lalit Kala Akademi National Exhibition award in 2006; later he won first prize in the 2009 Bhopal Biennale. In the 2007 exhibition, one painting depicted a crucified Christ with explicit genitals and a toilet beneath the cross; another, entitled 'Durga Mata', was of a nude woman attacking, with a trident (the weapon of Shiva), a baby issuing from her womb. Christian leaders lodged protests against the first painting, and a group of Hindu chauvinist activists belonging to the VHP (Vishwa Hindu Parishad) and BJP (Bharatiya Janata Party) vandalized the exhibition and roughed up Chandramohan for the second painting.[22] (This group was led by Niraj Jain, who has been known to brandish a revolver and once threw eggs at the Gujarat education minister for including them in school midday meals.[23]) The police stood by and then arrested not the vandals but the artist. (He was later released.) When the acting Dean of the Faculty of Fine Arts, Shivaji Panikkar, refused to close down the exhibition, the Vice-Chancellor, Manoj Soni, suspended him. Panikkar, stating that he feared for his life, went into hiding. Students and spokespersons of the Indian art community held protests throughout India, claiming that the closing of the exhibition was a direct assault on the rights of freedom of expression.

In commenting on this event, the well-known editor, columnist and critic Anil Dharker remarked:

> What has made the artists come together in protest is that this attack isn't an isolated one, but one more in a series now increasing in both frequency and wantonness...The Mumbai Police stood by when Shiv Sainiks attacked cinema theatres showing a Deepa Mehta film [*Fire*, which showed a lesbian relationship in a middle-class Hindu family]...Recently, the Mumbai cops did some moral policing of their own, arresting young couples found in 'compromising position' (policespeak for young men and women having their arms around each other).[24]

Dharker went on to list several more instances, but even these few are representative of broad patterns of attacks by various Hindutva groups (whose members call themselves Hindutvavadis).

There has been an increasing number of campaigns against artists and writers who link Hindu deities with sexuality, or talk openly and frankly about sexuality. In 1996, Hindutvavadis began terrorizing M.F. Husain for his paintings of naked Hindu goddesses. In 2006, after death threats and legal cases, Husain, whom many regarded as India's greatest living artist, and who was then ninety-one years old, was forced into exile in Dubai; he died in London in 2011. Some Hindutvavadis forced Deepa Mehta to leave Varanasi, where she was making a film about the mistreatment of Hindu widows in Varanasi (*Water*, 2005).[25] In 2013, Rajnath Singh, leader of the BJP, and now India's home minister (since the BJP won the national elections in 2014), said in an interview to the *Telegraph* newspaper that 'homosexuality is an unnatural act and cannot be supported'. In October 2014, the chief minister of the state of Haryana was reported to have said, 'If a girl is dressed decently, a boy will not look at her in the wrong way...If [they] want freedom, why don't they just roam around naked? Freedom has to be limited. These short clothes are Western influences. Our country's tradition asks girls to dress decently.' In Bangalore, Bombay, Delhi and several other Indian cities, vigilante Right-wing Hindu groups like the Sri Ram Sena ('The Army of Lord Rama') routinely beat up young couples seen together in public and women who visit pubs, and vandalize shops that sell Valentine Day cards.

The Hindutvavadis often accuse the people whom they censor of being polluted by Western influences, while, ironically, many of the Hindutvavadis' own actions closely resemble censoring frenzies in the United States. But the Indian incidents are better seen as part of a separate logic of

Hindu Puritanism, which, as we have seen, has a long history of its own. When a group of students and artists at Baroda University attempted to stage a protest demonstration for Chandramohan at the Faculty of Fine Arts, they organized an exhibition of photographs taken from the explicitly erotic sculptures that adorn the temples at Khajuraho, in Madhya Pradesh.[26] In choosing Khajuraho, they were making an implicit historical statement: the art heritage of India is rich in erotic themes, of which the images on the Khajuraho temples (built between 900 and 1100 CE) are a famous example. What happened to that tradition? How did India get from there to the scandal in Baroda?

Nowadays, on the public scene, 'a Hindu-nationalist health minister can insist that the "Indian traditions" of abstinence and fidelity are more effective barriers against HIV than condoms; and...the 1860 Penal Code [still in effect] defines all extramarital sex as criminal'.[27] Many Hindus, in India but also increasingly in the American diaspora, advocate a sanitized, 'spiritual' form of Hinduism (and, in India, a nationalist and anti-Muslim form). For such Hindus, the problem is not (as it was for some liberal Indian intellectuals) how to explain how India lost its appreciation of eroticism but, on the contrary, how to maintain that Hinduism was always the pure-minded, anti-erotic, ascetic tradition that it actually became, for many upper-class Hindus, only in the nineteenth century.

One way to make this argument was to swing to the other side of the pendulum and blame the British not for *suppressing* Indian eroticism but for *causing* it. Under Nehru, the Indian government chose to retain a British colonial era penal code of sexual repression, forbidding several acts 'against nature'—

acts that Nehru condemned by saying, 'such vices in India were due to Western influence'.[28] The irony is that in aping the British scorn for Indian sexuality, contemporary Hindus who favour censorship are letting foreign ideas about Hinduism triumph over and drive out native Hindu ideas about—and pride in—their own religion and in the diversity and tolerance that have always characterized the world of the mind in Hinduism. Among the other bad habits they picked up from the West, from seeds sown, perhaps, during colonization but flowering only in the more recent contacts with American imperialism, was the Protestant habit of censorship. Never before has the old tension between the erotic and ascetic strains of Hinduism taken the form of one path telling the other path that it has no right to exist.

## THE REBIRTH OF KAMA

But kama, which is to say the India of the ancient erotic past, is not so easily stamped out. Even in the nineteenth century, most Hindus continued cheerfully on the path that celebrated the earthier aspects of life. And now they live on in 'a reported two-thirds of young adults who would have casual, pre-marital sex before an arranged marriage',[29] and who, since 1991, can buy condoms called *KamaSutra*—and chocolate-, vanilla- and strawberry-flavoured condoms, too, marketed freely on Indian television channels. Through all this, many hundreds of folk songs and stories—often sung or told by women—have remained robustly bawdy. Clearly the attempt to transform the culture of the *Kamasutra* into what many people, Hindus and non-Hindus alike, mistakenly refer to as the *Karmasutra* (presumably a Vedantic text about reincarnation) has not succeeded.

But reports of the death of Kama have been, as Mark Twain famously said of his own death, greatly exaggerated. Kama is incarnate in a god who, like his Greek and Roman counterparts Eros and Cupid, enflames passion by shooting lovers with arrows of desire. And this Kama was indeed killed, but not permanently. In a poem entitled 'The Birth of the Prince',[30] by Kalidasa, often regarded as the greatest poet of ancient India (he probably lived in the fifth century), Kama tried to shoot an arrow at the god Shiva at a time when Shiva was deeply engrossed in ascetic meditation. Shiva opened his third eye and burnt Kama to ashes. But by destroying Kama's body, Shiva actually infused him into a number of other substances that worked Kama's magic even more effectively—moonlight, the arched brows of beautiful women, and so forth. I find this an encouraging metaphor for the unofficial thriving of movements that public censorship forces underground.

And it gets better. Later, when Shiva had fallen in love with Parvati, the exquisitely beautiful daughter of the mountain Himalaya, and had married her, he was in a rather different mood. Now when Rati, the wife of Kama and the incarnation of pleasure, begged Shiva to resuscitate her husband, the god granted her wish. (Kalidasa then describes the union of Shiva and Parvati in a canto so erotic that many later, more prudish scholars refuse to accept it as a genuine part of the poem.) I find this poem a persuasive and hopeful scenario for the revival of the *Kamasutra*, and the ultimate flourishing of its joyous spirit, in India.

# NOTES

## INTRODUCTION: REEDEEMING THE *KAMASUTRA*

1. *Kamasutra* 2.2.6-7. The editions I am using are *Arthashastra* of Kautilya (critical edition. Ed. R. P. Kangle. Bombay: University of Bombay, 1960); *Kamasutra* of Vatsyayana, with the commentary of Yashodhara. (Edited with the Hindi 'Jaya' commentary by Devadatta Shastri. Kashi Sanskrit Series 29. Chaukhambha Sanskrit Sansthan, Varanasi.) Unless otherwise noted, I will cite Patrick Olivelle's translation of the *Arthashastra* (*King, Governance, and Law in Ancient India: Kautilya's* Arthashastra and my own translation (with Sudhir Kakar) of the *Kamasutra*. A New Annotated Translation by Patrick Olivelle. Oxford: Oxford University Press, 2013). The one change I have made is to leave dharma, artha, and kama in Sanskrit rather than translating them in English, as the two cited translations do.
2. *The Kamasutra of Vatsyayana*. A new translation, introduction, and commentary. With Sudhir Kakar. London and New York: Oxford World Classics, 2002. 231 pp.
3. It has been translated into Italian (translation by Vincenzo Vergiani, Milan: Adelphi Edizione, 2003; reprint, 2010), Norwegian (Oslo: Kagge Forlag, 2004), German (translation by Robin Cackett, Berlin: Verlag Klaus Wagenbach, 2004; paperback, 2008), Latvian (translation by Andzela Suvajeva, Riga: Zvaigzne ABC, 2004), Spanish (translation by Mariano Vazquez, Madrid: EDAF, 2005), and French (translation by Alain Porte, Paris: Seuil, 2007; Sagesses, 2010). A Portuguese translation is forthcoming.
4. Manu (*Manusmriti*. Bombay: Bharatiya Vidya Series, 1972-8) 3.45-49.
5. Manu 5.161-4 and 8.352-378; *Arthashastra* 3.3-4.

6. Manu 8.371-2.
7. And the *Arthashastra* tells you how to smoke out the guilty couple: 'Adultery is indicated by the caressing of each other's hair; or else by circumstantial evidence of carnal enjoyment, through experts in these matters, or through the woman's confession.' AS 4.12.36.
8. AS 4.12.34.
9. KS 5.6.46-48.

## 1. THE STRANGE AND THE FAMILIAR IN THE *KAMASUTRA*

1. This chapter is a much revised combination of several published articles: 'The *Kamasutra*: It isn't *All* about Sex' in the *Kenyon Review*, 2003; 'Reading the *Kamasutra*: The Strange and the Familiar' in *Daedalus*, 2007; 'On the *Kamasutra*' in *Daedalus*, 2002; 'Other Peoples' Religions, Other Peoples' *Kama* and *Karma*' in *The Stranger's Religion: Fascination and Fear*, ed. Anna Lanstrom (Notre Dame, Indiana. Notre Dame University Press, 2004); and *La Trappola della Giumenta* (Milan: Adelphi Edizione, 2003).
2. The *Kamasutra* must have been written after 225 CE because the western Indian political situation that Vatsyayana describes shows the Abhiras and the Andhras ruling simultaneously over a region that had been ruled by the Andhras alone until 225 CE. Its style seems very close to that of the *Arthashastra*, also of uncertain date, but generally placed in the second century CE; it cites the *Arthashastra* explicitly at 1.2.10, and implicitly elsewhere. The fact that the text does not mention the Guptas, who ruled North India from the beginning of the fourth century CE, suggests that the text predates that period. The *Kamasutra* is mentioned by name in the *Vasavadatta* of Subandhu, composed under Chandragupta Vikramaditya, who reigned at the beginning of the fifth century CE.
3. 'The Cosmo Kamasutra', *Cosmopolitan*, September 1998; 'The Cosmo Kamasutra, #2', *Cosmopolitan*, September 1999, 256–259.

4. Roland Barthes, *The Pleasure of the Text*. New York: Hill and Wang, 1975.
5. Yashodhara on the *Kamasutra* 1.4.1. Henceforth, all citations of numbered verses without other attributions are from the *Kamasutra*, and Y will designate Yashodhara.
6. 1.5.1.
7. 3.5.5.
8. 2.10.22-25.
9. 1.4.2.
10. 1.4.31-33.
11. 1.4.5-7.
12. 1.4.8-13.
13. These stories were collected in *The Ocean of Story* (*Kathasaritsagara*) in about the tenth century.
14. 1.4.29-30.
15. 1.3.15.
16. 1.3.16.
17. 2.8.4-5.
18. 3.4.9.
19. 5.4.54.
20. 2.2.89.
21. 4.1.9.
22. 3.4.6.
23. 6.2.1-73.
24. 6.3.27-35.
25. 1.5.12-14.
26. 2.8.25-29.
27. 2.6.23-33.
28. 2.9.41.
29. 7.2.55.
30. 2.4.25.

## 2. THE KAUTILYAN *KAMASUTRA*

1. Y on KS 1.1.2.
2. For Pururavas and Urvashi, see *Rig Veda* 10.95 (Wendy Doniger

O'Flaherty, *The Rig Veda: An Anthology, 108 Hymns Translated from the Sanskrit.* Harmondsworth: Penguin Classics, 1981, 253-6); *Shatapatha Brahmana* (Benares: Chowkhamba Sanskrit Series, 1964, 11.5.1.1-17; Wendy Doniger O'Flaherty, *Women, Androgynes, and Other Mythical Beasts* (Chicago: University of Chicago Press, 1980); and Wendy Doniger, *Splitting the Difference: Gender and Myth in Ancient Greece and India* (Chicago and London: University of London Press and University of Chicago Press, 1999).

3. Y on 1.2.41.
4. It can also be translated as goal or aim (as in the three aims of human life), gain (versus loss), money, the meaning of a word, and the purpose of something.
5. From *kutila*, 'crooked'.
6. The KS cites the AS explicitly at 1.2.10.
7. 1.2.9-10.
8. Moreover, the KS calls the AS 'The Tasks of the Superintendent', the name of a preexisting source, the *Adhyakshapracara,* which may predate Kautilya by a century or more and which forms the bulk of Book Two of the extant text of the AS.
9. *Charaka Samhita* 1.1.14.3-34.
10. Manu 4.214-16.
11. Manu 12.44-45.
12. Manu 8.362-3.
13. Plato had a similar problem with them.
14. AS 7.17.34-39.
15. Manu 6.33-86.
16. In much the manner, Romeo and Juliet employed Friar Lawrence.
17. AS 1.1.1.
18. 1.1.3.
19. 1.19-12.
20. There are nine: two general editors (Shvetaketu Auddalaki and Babhravya of Panchala) and the individual editors of each of the seven books: Charayana, Suvarnanabha, Ghotakamukha,

Gonardiya, Gonikaputra, Dattaka, and Kuchumara. The texts cited here no longer exist, but may have existed at the time of Vatsyayana, since he and, later, Yashodhara often quote directly from them.

21. AS 1.17.4-43. There he names Bharadvaja, Vishalaksha, Parashara, Pishuna, Kaunapadanta, Vatavyadhi, and the Ambhiyas.
22. AS 1.8.1-29. Here the same group testifies, one by one, in the same order, except that the Ambhiyas are replaced by Bahudantiputra.
23. 1.5.22-26.
24. AS 1.20.1, 10-13.
25. 1.4.1-4.
26. AS 13.1.1-3.
27. 3.1.6.
28. AS 4.13.28.
29. 4.1.19-21.
30. AS 14.2.6-8, 14.3.1.
31. 5.6.24-25, 7.1.
32. AS 14.3.5-8-14.
33. AS 14.2.6-8 and KS 7.2.41, 47.
34. AS 1.14.1-6.
35. 5.1.50-54.
36. 1.5.5-21; 5.1.21-42.
37. 5.1.17-42.
38. AS 6.2.38; cf. also 7.15.12; 9.2.3- 6; 9.3.39; 9.4.8.
39. AS 1.16 and throughout the book; KS 1.5.35-6, 3.4.32-33, 3.5.1-11, 3.5.19-27, 5.4.
40. AS 2.7.9-10.
41. 5.1.17-42.
42. 5.1.43-49.
43. AS 7.6.23-37.
44. 6.4.3-37.
45. AS 1.6.5-6.
46. AS 1.17.28-33.
47. AS 1.17.34-38.

48. AS 1.10.3-12. The Hindus generally formulated a group of three emotions, usually desire, anger, and greed (*Bhavagad Gita* 7.101.14) or, occasionally, desire, anger and fear. But they often added a fourth, metaphysical, epistemological emotion: delusion (*moha).* The *Arthashastra* speaks of desire, anger, and greed (the original triad) plus pride, conceit, and excitement, as the 'six enemies'.
49. AS 1.10.7-8.
50. AS 1.10. 13.
51. 5.6.40-42.
52. AS 1.20.21. Olivelle renders *varshadhara* here as 'eunuch' but I don't think there were eunuchs in harems at this time, and so I prefer to render the term 'celibate'.
53. AS 1.17.2.
54. AS 1.20.14-17.
55. AS 1.10.18-19.
56. In this case it is the Ambhiyas.
57. 5.6.43-44.
58. Manu 4.145-6; 6.86, 92; and many other places.
59. Lorraine Daston, personal communication, September 14, 2014.
60. AS 1.6.1, 3-4.
61. AS 1.7.1.
62. AS 1.16.18-23.
63. AS 1.15.11.
64. AS 1.6.4-12
65. 1.2.34-36.
66. 1.2.37.
67. AS 8.3.15.
68. 3 1.2.
69. 5.5.37.
70. 5.5.28-9.
71. 2.7.28-30.
72. Manu 4.127.
73. 1.5.8-21.
74. Manu 3.27-34.
75. AS 3.2.1-10.

76. 3.5.1-27.
77. 3.5.29.
78. Manu 3.35.
79. 3.5.28.
80. AS 2.27.28; 1.3.15.
81. AS 4.13 41.
82. 5.6.3.
83. AS 4.12.36-40.
84. 5.4.42.
85. AS 3.2.31.
86. 1.5.30.
87. AS 1.6.2.
88. 1.2.11-12.
89. 2.7.1.
90. 2.5.27. 31.
91. 2.7.1-21.
92. 2.4, 5, and 7.
93. This was not the only paradigm of sexual love, however. A more romantic view, of two people who fall in love and remain true to one another through various calamities was also fully developed in classical India, most famously in the stories of Rama and Sita in the *Ramayana*, and Nala and Damayanti in the *Mahabharata*, and in many subsequent works.
94. The torch song, 'Mean to Me', recorded by Annette Hanshaw in 1929.
    Music by Fred E. Ahlert and lyrics by Roy Turk, 1929.
    You're mean to me
    Why must you be mean to me?
    Gee, honey, it seems to me
    You love to see me cryin'.

    I don't know why
    I stay home each night
    When you say you'll phone
    You don't and I'm left alone.
    Singing the blues and sighin'.

You treat me coldly
Each day in the year
You always scold me
Whenever somebody is near, dear

It must be great fun to be mean to me
You shouldn't, for can't you see
What you mean to me?

95. Nina Paley, 'The Sitayana, or, Sita Sings the Blues'.

## 3. THE MYTHOLOGY OF THE *KAMASUTRA*

1. This chapter is a much revised version of an essay published in *The Anthropologist and the Native: Essays for Gananath Obeyesekere* (ed. H.L. Seneviratne: Firenze: Societa Editrice Florentina; Delhi, Manohar, 2009).
2. 1.1.5-10.
3. Y on 1.1.8.
4. Y on 1.1.9.
5. *Mahabharata* 1.113.9-20.
6. 1.1.11.
7. Y on 1.1.11.
8. Wendy Doniger, *Splitting the Difference: Gender and Myth in Ancient Greece and India* (Chicago: The University of Chicago Press, 1999), 260-280.
9. 1.1.9-14.
10. Wendy Doniger, 'Echoes of the *Mahabharata*: Why is a Parrot the Narrator of the *Bhagavata Purana* and the *Devibhagavata Purana*?' In Wendy Doniger, ed., *Purana Perennis* (Albany: State University of New York Press, 1993), 31-57.
11. *Introduction to the Jataka* 1.68; trans. Warren, *Buddhism in Translation*, 71-2.
12. 2.6.11.
13. 1.2.29.
14. Y on 1.2.29.
15. 2.10.12.

16. Y on 2.10;12.
17. Wendy Doniger, *The Implied Spider: Politics and Theology in Myth*. New York: Columbia University Press, 1998; second edition, 2010.
18. 3.5.5.
19. 5.4.14.
20. *Mahabharata* 1.64-69.
21. Kalidasa, *Abhijnanasakuntalam*.
22. Y on 5.4.14.
23. 1.2.34-36.
24. Y on 1.2.36.
25. 5.4.14.
26. Y on 5.4.14.
27. *Kathasaritsagara*112.89.
28. Jeffrey Masson, 'A Note on the Sources of Bhasa's (?) Vimaraka.'*Journal of the Oriental Institute of Baroda*, XIX, September-December 1965, nos. 1-2, 60-74.
29. A good precedent for this telling of stories whose actual morals seem diametrically opposed to their supposed and intended morals appears in the *Mahabharata*. There, Satyavati tells several stories to her two daughters-in-law to persuade them to allow themselves to be impregnated by Vyasa, the brother of their dead husband, in order to continue the line. But the stories she tells, about women similarly officially impregnated by men other than their husbands, in fact result in disastrous births; one of them is born blind, as, indeed, will be the fate of the son of one of Satyavati's daughters-in-law. *Mahabharata* 1.98-100.
30. Y on 6.1.17.
31. Y on 1.2.36.
32. *Mahabharata* 4.21.1-67, with a verse omitted from the critical edition after 4.21.46.
33. 1.5.30.
34. Y on 1.2.35.
35. 1.2.41.
36. Doniger, *Splitting the Difference*.
37. 2.7.28-30.

38. Y on 2.7.28-30.
39. 5.5.29.
40. Y on 5.5.29.
41. 5.5.1-2.
42. 5.5.1-4.

## 4. WOMEN IN THE *KAMASUTRA*

1. This chapter is revised from an essay that was written for *Indologica: T. Ya. Elizarenkova Memorial Volume*, Book 2, ed. L. Kulikor (Moskva, 2012), 207-224; combined with 'Lost in Translation: Gender in the *Kamasutra*', in *The Magazine*, 2002.
2. There is also a *Kama Sutra for Cats* (by Mrs Woodhouse, of 'good dog' fame).
3. 1.3.1-11.
4. 3.4.36-47.
5. 1.1.11.
6. AS 3.2.31.
7. 1.5.30.
8. AS 3.2.14.
9. AS 3.2.19-34.
10. 4.1.1-41.
11. Manu 4.150.
12. Manu 9.10-11.
13. 3.2.35 and 4.2.31-5.
14. 5.4.42.
15. 2.8.17-18.
16. Yashodhara's commentary on 2.1.30.
17. 2.1.23-30.
18. 2.8.16.
19. Sir Richard Francis Burton, *The Kama Sutra of Vatsyayana: The Classic Hindu Treatise on Love and Social Conduct* (Introduction by John W. Spellman. New York: E. P. Dutton & Co, Inc, 1962), p. 121.
20. 3.2.35 and 4.2.31-5.
21. Manu 5.154.

22. 4.1.19-21.
23. 1.5.22.
24. 4.2.31-4.
25. 1.2.20.
26. Manu 9.12-17.
27. 5.1.8.
28. 5.1.23, 25-6, 28-9, 31-35, 37-41.
29. 5.1.43.
30. 6.3.39-44.
31. James C. Scott, *Weapons of the Weak* and *Domination and the Arts of Resistance*.
32. 5.1.51-4.
33. Doniger, *The Implied Spider*, chapter five.
34. 5.5.7-10.

## 5. THE THIRD NATURE: GENDER INVERSIONS IN THE *KAMASUTRA*

1. This chapter is revised from an essay that was written for *Indologica: T. Ya. Elizarenkova Memorial Volume*, Book 2, ed. Kulikor, L. (Moskva, 2012), 207-224; combined with 'Lost in Translation: Gender in the *Kamasutra*', in *The Magazine*, 2002.
2. 2.1.10.
3. 2.7.22.
4. *Rig Veda* 10.129.5.
5. 2.6.17.
6. 2.7.23.
7. 2.8.6.
8. 2.8. 39.
9. *Amarushataka*, verse 89.
10. Thanks to Blake Wentworth for bringing this commentary to my attention and translating it.
11. Manu 11.174.
12. AS 3.18.4.
13. Mary Douglas, *Purity and Danger: An Analysis of Concepts of Pollution and Taboo*. London: Routledge and K. Paul, 1966.

14. *Bhagavad Gita* 2.3.
15. 2.9.1-5.
16. 2.9.6-11.
17. 2.2. 27-8.
18. 2.3. 31.
19. 2.1. 42.
20. 3.2.3.
21. 3.2.4-6.
22. 2.1.26.
23. 1.5.27.
24. 1.5.27.
25. Serena Nanda, *Neither Man Nor Woman: The Hijras of India*. Belmont, CA: Wadsworth Pub. Co., 1990.
26. Fawn M. Brodie, *The Devil Drives: A Life of Sir Richard Burton* (New York: Ballantine, 1967), 369.
27. William G. Archer, Preface to the *Kama Sutra* ( London: George Allen and Unwin, 1963), 17.
28. Brodie, 370.
29. 5.6.2-4.
30. 5.6.2.
31. 7.1.20.
32. Manu 8.369-70, AS 4.12.20-22.
33. 5.6.1-4.
34. 2.8.41.
35. 5.4.15.
36. *Buddhacharita of Ashvaghosha* (Ed. E.H. Johnston. Calcutta: Punjab University Oriental Publications, 1935-6). 4.12.
37. 2.9.35-36.
38. 1.1.11.

## 6. THE MARE'S TRAP: THE NATURE AND CULTURE OF SEX

1. This chapter is based on the text of a book first published in Italian and subsequently published in French and Spanish, but never in English: *Trappola della Giumenta*. Trans. Vicenzo

Vergiani. Milan: Adelphi Edizione, 2003. Also: *Le Kama Sutra de Bikaner*. Trans. Fabienne Durand-Bogaert. Paris: Gallimard, 2004. *La trampa de la Yegua*. Traducción de Damián Alou. Barcelona: Editorial Anagrama, 2004.

2. 2.1.1.
3. 2.6.1, 7.
4. 7.2.37.
5. 2.1.1.3-4.
6. 2.1.1.
7. Sir Richard Francis Burton. [*Anangaranga*]. *The Hindu Art of Love (Ars Amoris Indica) or Ananga-Ranga (Stage of the Bodiless One)*. Translated from the Sanskrit of Kalyana Malla and annotated by A. F. F. and B. F. R. Privately issued by the British Bibliophiles' Society. 1907. [1885].
8. 2.1.5-8, 30-31.
9. 2.7.11.
10. 2.1.19.
11. For the story of Chudala, from the *Yogavasistha*, see Wendy Doniger, *Dreams, Illusion, and Other Realities* (Chicago: The University of Chicago Press, 1984) and Wendy Doniger, *Splitting the Difference: Gender and Myth in Ancient Greece and India* (Chicago: The University of Chicago Press, 1999), pp. 287-292.
12. 2.1.36.
13. Y on 2.1.14.
14. 2.1.11, 12, 15, 16.
15. 2.8.24.
16. Y on 2.1.4.
17. 2.1.3, 6.
18. 7.2.1.
19. 2.1.3, 6.
20. 7.2.36.
21. 7.1.25-30.
22. 7.1.25, 27, 28.
23. An undergraduate woman said this in a class I was teaching on the *Kamasutra*.

24. 7.2.14-24.
25. 7.2.25-27.
26. 2.6.12.
27. 2.6.8, 10-11.
28. 2.6.8-9.
29. Y on 2.6.9.
30. 2.6. 13-20.
31. 2.8.33.
32. See Wendy Doniger, 'The Mythology of Horses in India', pp. 438-451 of *On Hinduism* (Delhi: Aleph Book Company, 2014).
33. See Wendy Doniger, 'The Submarine Mare in the Mythology of Shiva', pp. 452-472 of *On Hinduism.*
34. 2.1.24.
35. *Jaiminiya Brahmana* 1.161-163. Wendy Doniger O'Flaherty, *Tales of Sex and Violence: Folklore, Sacrifice, and Danger in the Jaiminiya Brahmana* (Chicago: University of Chicago Press, 1985), p. 101.
36. 2.7.1-21.
37. 1.3.15, 1.4.8, 6.1.15.
38. 2.8.27-29.
39. Jon Spayde, 'The Politically Correct *Kama Sutra*'. In *The Utne Reader*, November-December 1996, p. 57.
40. 1.2.16-20.
41. Y on 1.4.4.
42. Y on 1.4.4.
43. 2.10.1-4.
44. 2.10.7-8.
45. 2.10.6, 9-13.

## 7. THE RISE AND FALL OF KAMA AND THE *KAMASUTRA*

1. This chapter is loosely based on part of an article entitled 'From Kama to Karma: The Resurgence of Puritanism in Contemporary India', originally published in *Social Research*: *India's World*, vol. 78, no. 1, Spring 2011, eds. Arien Mack and Arjun Appadurai, pp. 49-74. Reprinted as pp.47-70 of *India's World:*

*The Politics of Creativity in a Globalized Society* (New Delhi: Raintree, 2012), and later reprinted in my volume *On Hinduism* (Delhi: Aleph Book Company, 2014).

2. *Rig Veda* 10.129.4.
3. *Brihad Aranyaka Upanishad* 6.2.13, 6.4.3.
4. David Gordon White, *Kiss of the Yogini: "Tantric Sex" in its South Asian Contexts* (Chicago: University of Chicago Press, 2003), 220.
5. Yigal Bronner, *Extreme Poetry: The South Asian Movement of Simultaneous Narration (*New York: Columbia University Press, 2010).
6. A.K. Ramanujan,Velcheru Narayana Rao and David Shulman, *When God is a Customer* (Berkeley, Los Angeles, London: University of California Press, 1994), 117-18.
7. Bombay (Presidency) Supreme Court. *Report of the Maharaj Libel Case: And of the Bhattia Conspiracy Case* (Bombay: Bombay Gazette Press, 1862), 213.
8. James McConnachie, *The Book of Love: In Search of the Kamasutra* (London: Atlantic, 2007),197-8.
9. V. S. Naipaul, *Half a Life* (New York: Vintage Books, 2002), 110.
10. McConnachie, *The Book of Love*, 197-8.
11. McConnachie, *The Book of Love*, 55, 57.
12. McConnachie, *The Book of Love*, 197-8.
13. McConnachie, *The Book of Love*, 194.
14. Fawn M. Brodie, *The Devil Drives: A Life of Sir Richard Burton*) New York: Ballantine, 1967), 358.
15. William G. Archer, Preface to the *Kama Sutra* (London: George Allen and Unwin, 1963), 36.
16. Brodie, *The Devil Drives*, 357.
17. KS 2.7.20.
18. Burton, *The Kama Sutra*, 117-18.
19. KS 4.1.19-21.
20. Burton, *The Kama Sutra*, 160.
21. Vikram Chandra, *Love and Longing in Bombay* (Boston: Little, Brown and Company, 1997), 126.

22. Binoy Valsan, 'Baroda Art student's work stirs up religious controversy'. *Rediff India Abroad*, May 10, 2007.
23. Anil Dharker, 'Beauty And the Beast: Baroda episode underscores threat to creative expression.' *Mainstream* 45: 23 (May 25, 2007).
24. Dharker, 'Beauty And the Beast'.
25. Richard Philips and and Waruna Alahakoon. 'Hindu chauvinists block filming of Deepa Mehta's *Water.' World Socialist Web Site*, 12 February, 2000.
26. Sandhya Bordewekar, Interview with Shivaji K. Panikkar and Chandramohan. *Art India*, 12:3 (2007), 61-67; here, 62.
27. McConnachie, *The Book of Love*, 288.
28. McConnachie, *The Book of Love*, 209.
29. McConnachie, *The Book of Love*, 229.
30. Kalidasa, *Kumarasambhava*.